INTRODUCTION
by Winka Dubbeldam, Chair

I am happy to present this new issue of *Pressing Matters* to you, our eighth edition, and to share great news: thanks to the generous support of Stuart Weitzman, PennDesign is now the Stuart Weitzman School of Design. This opens up a vast array of opportunities for the Department of Architecture that we are excited to implement in the coming years.

To give you an idea of more recent accomplishments, our Robotics Lab is now in full operation mode and new robotics courses are incorporated into our curriculum. We are on the brink of launching the MSD with a con-centration in *Robotics and Automated Systems* (MSD-RAS), our third MSD program, directed by Assistant Professor Robert Stuart-Smith. This is an exciting addition to our already existing programs: the MSD-EBD directed by Professor of Architecture Bill Braham and the MSD-AAD directed by Professor of Architecture Ali Rahim.

We are proud of our students, whose work continues to earn important awards and recognition. Alexandra Adamski, a second-year Master of Architecture student, won the inaugural $50,000 Kanter Tritsch Prize in Energy and Architectural Innovation, funded by Weitzman School alumna Lori Kanter Tritsch and Wharton alumnus William P. Lauder. Noting it as a "life-changing" award, Adamski says it won't only impact her financial situation, but also her creativity and professional plans upon graduation. Weitzman School alum-nus Gary Polk (MArch'18) was awarded a 2019 Archiprix International Hunter Douglas Award in Santiago, Chile. His design, *Synthetic Cultures*, was one of seven finalists out of 407 nominees from around the world. He was the only representative from the United States. Of Polk's work, the jury said, "The nar-rative is a wonderful "sci-fi" project. Not every project has to be plausible, and this one takes you out of your comfort zone." Associate Professor Simon Kim served as an advisor for *Synthetic Cultures*. We are thankful for the great support of our alumni that stay connected to the Department in many ways.

Architectural Theory Now, a symposium organized by Associate Professor Franca Trubiano and Professor David Leatherbarrow of the Weitzman School and Peter Laurence of Clemson University, asked some important questions, such as "Is Architectural Theory M.I.A., D.O.A. or simply in transition?" The panels Within/Without, Practices, and Re-Definitions further discussed these issues from April 4-6 at the Weitzman School of Design. The organizers con-cluded: "If little in architectural theory, as developed in recent decades, has prepared architects to thoughtfully engage in our contemporary challenges, it is perhaps time to make a new start in defining architectural theory now."

The publication of *57 Pavilions* documents three years of architectural design research at the Weitzman School. It examines new potentials for

20

University of Pennsylvania Stuart Weitzman School of Design
Department of Architecture
212 Meyerson Hall
210 S. 34th Street
Philadelphia, PA 19104-6311
215.898.5728

www.design.upenn.edu/architecture/graduate/info
archdept@design.upenn.edu

20

part-to-whole assemblies where experiments in material expression, morphology, performance, and culture fuse with advanced digital design processes and fabrication to produce full-scale architectural "prototypes." Edited by Associate Professor of Architecture Andrew Saunders, it combines faculty texts with rigorous student design-research projects in this exhilarating book published by ORO. Our students also publish: the inaugural issue of student magazine *Babble* was released in February and focuses on *Identity Crisis*, featuring texts by the students on Abstraction, Subversion, and Realism, and interviews with Thom Mayne, Masoud Akbarzedah, Philip Block, and Carrie Norman and Nate Hume, among others.

We will continue our focus on excellence in design, rigorous research, and social equity. We created a study plan that elaborates on the expanded role of the architect, beyond that of the designer, where the architect is considered an expert, a rigorous researcher, and a team leader. In a time of food and water scarcity and environmental and climate challenges, we train our students to be active participants in the global discourse towards a better, safer, and cleaner world. We pride ourselves on the inclusion of diverse external experts, not only in our design studios, but also through annual symposia, weekly lectures, and regular design reviews. Our vast group of visiting critics add to our own dedicated and talented faculty, that every year challenge us to think harder, move faster and create a better world. They add to the dialogue and bring the discourse of architecture further.

Pressing Matters is published by ORO Editions and designed by the renowned office WSDIA. We hope that this publication will help integrate you into the ongoing investigations and discussions at the Department of Architecture, and that you will visit us in the near future.

Winka Dubbeldam, Assoc. AIA
Miller Professor and Chair
Department of Architecture
Stuart Weitzman School of Design

UNIVERSITY OF PENNSYLVANIA NAMES SCHOOL OF DESIGN IN RECOGNITION OF STUART WEITZMAN'S LIFETIME COMMITMENT AND SUPPORT OF PENN

The University of Pennsylvania School of Design has been renamed in honor of award-winning designer and footwear icon Stuart Weitzman, Wharton Class of 1963, in recognition of both his ongoing philanthropic support of the University and his active engagement in its academic activities. The new name, the University of Pennsylvania Stuart Weitzman School of Design, reflects Weitzman's enduring influence in the world of design and his extraordinary support of the School.

"Stuart has been an inspiration to the thousands of students with whom he has connected in large lecture and smaller classroom settings, and through one-on-one conversations," Penn President Amy Gutmann said. "His lifelong support of the University and the School of Design truly aligns his own body of work in design with his ongoing commitment to Penn in the most meaningful and impactful way.

"Stuart's inspiring example will enhance the School's competitive position by enabling it to attract and support the highest-caliber students, strengthen its signature programs, and elevate its stature among the world's premier schools of design."

In addition, the School's central plaza, located adjacent to College Green between Meyerson Hall and Fisher Fine Arts Library, will be named The Stuart Weitzman Plaza and will undergo significant redesign and renovation in the upcoming months by renowned landscape architect, Laurie Olin, Practice Professor Emeritus of Landscape Architecture at the School of Design.

Stuart Weitzman, who graduated from the Wharton School at the University of Pennsylvania in 1963, is one of the most recognizable names in luxury designer footwear. He founded his eponymous company in 1986. In the ensuing decades, he built Stuart Weitzman into one of the world's most renowned fashion footwear brands.

"What makes Stuart Weitzman so inspiring is his rock-solid belief that investing in people and education is the way to make a lasting impact," said Dean and Paley Professor Frederick Steiner. "From this day forward, the inter-related fields that comprise design at Penn will be linked with the name and design legacy of Stuart Weitzman. Our School is enormously proud to bear his name."

NAME CHANGE

Stuart Weitzman

AUGUST 2018

NEW FACULTY

Dorit Aviv joins the architecture faculty as a lecturer. Currently a PhD candidate at Princeton University, she is a designer and researcher specializing in the fields of energy and ecology; her work investigates the relationships between thermodynamics, geometry and material science. She has taught at The Cooper Union, Pratt Institute, and Princeton University and has practiced design at Tod Williams Billie Tsien Architects, KPF New York and Shanghai, and Atelier Raimund Abraham. She also curated the energy pavilion in the 2017 Seoul Biennale for Architecture and Urbanism along with Forrest Meggers. Aviv earned a BArch at The Cooper Union, and an MArch and certificate in urban planning from Princeton University's School of Architecture and Woodrow Wilson School of Public Policy.

Sophie Debiasi Hochhäusl is an assistant professor for architectural history and theory in the Department of Architecture. In the past year, Hochhäusl was the Frieda L. Miller Fellow at the Radcliffe Institute for Advanced Study at Harvard University. Her scholarly work centers on modern architecture and urban culture in Austria, Germany, and the United States, with a focus on the history of social movements, environmental history, and women's and gender studies.

Hochhäusl is the recipient of the Carter Manny Award by the Graham Foundation, the Bruno Zevi Award, and the Clearance Stein Fellowship in Landscape and Urban Studies. She received an MArch from the Academy of Fine Arts Vienna, and an MA and PhD from Cornell University in History of Architecture and Urbanism.

In other faculty transitions, Daniel Barber, associate professor of architecture, and Andrew Saunders, associate professor of architecture, earned tenure.

After 22 productive and rewarding years as chair of the Graduate Group in Architecture, David Leatherbarrow, professor of architecture, has decided to devote himself full-time to teaching and scholarship; he is succeeded by Daniel Barber.

IN SHANGHAI, CELEBRATING ARCHITECTURAL GIANTS WITH PHILLY ROOTS

The Weitzman School of Design is widely recognized in China, not only for training the next generation of designers and preservationists, but as the alma mater of the founders of modern architecture. Now, this first wave of Chinese alumni, which included the power couple Liang Sicheng (GAr'27) and Huiyin Lin (BFA'27), is the subject of a major traveling exhibition at the Shanghai Contemporary Art Museum.

Drawing on the collections of the Architectural Archives, *The Rise of Modernity: The First Generation of Chinese Architects from the University of Pennsylvania* focuses on 20 individuals who studied at the Weitzman School between 1918 and 1937.

Having been drawn to Philadelphia by charismatic faculty members like Paul Cret, they returned to China upon graduation to practice professionally, spreading out across the country. They designed office buildings, residences, schools, hospitals, theaters, and more.

The exhibition was curated by Tong Ming, a professor and director of Urban Design at the College of Architecture and Urban Planning, Tongji University.

Ming describes these early alumni as being "instrumental in the construction of the nation." Their contribution, he says, lay in their relentless search "for a design approach to emphasize both a new form of national identity and a modern style."

The exhibition is accompanied by a 107-page brochure that explores architectural education at the Weitzman School in the early 20th century and the rise of Shanghai—the birthplace of Chinese modernism in architecture—as well as the work of the architects themselves. In addition to Liang and Lin, Fan Wenzhao, designer of the Nanking Theater (today's Shanghai Concert Hall), Yang Tinbao, Ton Jun, and Chen Zhi are represented.

SEPTEMBER 2018

ASSET ARCHITECTURE 3 PUBLISHED

Asset Architecture 3 is the latest installment in the Department of Architecture series edited by Ali Rahim, professor of architecture and director of the Master of Science in Design with a concentration in Advanced Architectural Design (MSD-AAD) program.

The issue features student work from the MSD-AAD studios, including interviews and behind-the-scenes model production. The cover image is from the project "Vertical Mausoleum" by Bosung Jeon, Carrie Rose Frattali, and Xiaoyu Zhao.

The publication also includes essays by Matthew Soules, assistant professor, The University of British Columbia ('Form Against Finance?'); Robert Neumayr, lecturer, Weitzman School and assistant professor, University of Applied Arts, Vienna ('The Best Building Money Can Buy'); and Tom Verebes, provost, Turenscape Academy ('The Paradigms of Politics and Privatization - From Raymond Hood to Robin Hood').

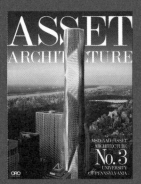

ROBOTICS LAB PUSHES BOUNDARIES OF DESIGN AND CONSTRUCTION FOR TINY HOUSE PROTOTYPE

The prototype, when it's finished, will be a one-to-one scale model of a tiny house, with the entire building envelope under 400 square feet. It will be made of concrete, with all finishes and furnishings—from sinks to shelving—built into the form. It will consist of about ten total pieces, which can be assembled and disassembled. Each piece will be cast inside a mold that will be cut by a robot in the ARI Robotics Lab, located in the basement of Meyerson Hall.

But that's about all that Robert Stuart-Smith and Masoud Akbarzadeh can say about the design at the moment. Stuart-Smith and Akbarzadeh are both assistant professors of architecture at the Weitzman School. Each runs a research group—the Autonomous Manufacturing Lab in Stuart-Smith's case, and the Polyhedral Structures Lab in Akbarzadeh's—that falls under the umbrella Advanced Research and Innovation Lab, led by Miller Professor and Chair of Architecture Winka Dubbeldam. Starting last year, with a gift from Penn alumnus Hanley Bodek (C'77) to support hands-on design and construction experience for students, Stuart-Smith and Akbarzadeh began work on a tiny house prototype to be displayed and open to the public. They've taught a seminar and a studio and enlisted more than two dozen student researchers in the project. If they're successful, the final result—they haven't committed to a completion date yet—will open a new chapter for housing that could be developed anywhere.

OCTOBER 2018

WEITZMAN SHOOL ALUMNUS WINS 'HOME: WHAT IS THE FUTURE?' COMPETITION

Dazhong Yi (MArch'18) received the Innovation Award from online research platform archoutloud.com. In "Home: What is the Future?" competitors were asked to consider "the impact of population shifts, the unpredictability of our changing ecosystem, contemporary forms of community housing and community relations, and newly engineered materials."

Yi's winning submission, titled "Above the Tire," was created in Volkan Alkanoglu's 704 Studio in Spring 2018:

"Above the Tire" combines the technological advances of self-driving cars with microscale living. In cities like Los Angeles, the proposed site for the prototype structure, this form of housing could revolutionize the relationship between the vehicle and the home, and maximizing the benefit of this form of new technology."

WINKA DUBBELDAM DESIGNS ASIAN GAMES SPORTS PARK

Miller Professor and Chair of Architecture Winka Dubbeldam's firm, Archi-Tectonics, won the Asian Games 2022 Sports Park Competition in Hangzhou, China. The project includes a 115 acre park designed with !Melk landscape architects, two stadiums, a shopping mall, and a fitness and visitor center. The park will open in March 2021.

The project was also featured in the AEDES exhibit: "Archi-Tectonics / Winka Dubbeldam & Justin Korhammer, New York. Flat Lands & Massive Things – From NL to NYC & Beyond," which opened on March 15, 2019 in Berlin.

Designed to be a simple "Big L" of 5 x 5 x 5 m, it documents how the influences of Dubbeldam's Dutch-American background are consciously or unconsciously reflected in her work. The exhibition also provided insight into the creative working methods of Archi-Tectonics, combining the use of the newest digital technologies with philosophical approaches. Arch-Tectonics is known for its use of hybrid sustainable materials and smart building systems. For the exhibition, Abet Laminati products created the custom "Big L" exhibition display, made with Metalleido and MEG panels customized with the digital printing technology. The exhibition opening included

a panel discussion on smart manufacturing called "Don't Tell Me It Can't Be Done."

NOVEMBER 2018

ANDREW SAUNDERS' BAROQUE TOPOLOGIES AT UNIVERSITY OF ARKANSAS

An exhibition of work from Associate Professor Andrew Saunders' "Baroque Topologies" research was on display at the University of Arkansas. It was designed by Saunders with graduate architecture students Kurt Nelson and Ariel Cooke-Zamora. The exhibition was presented by the Fay Jones School of Architecture and Design and was on view in Vol Walker Hall.

In his "Baroque Topologies" research, Saunders explores how emerging technology—including high-resolution 3D digital scanning and printing—provide unprecedented access to Baroque architecture's formal complexities, intricate detail, and deep topological structure. His field research in Rome and Turin, Italy documents the most significant Baroque works. This archive will be an extremely valuable worldwide resource for advancing contemporary teaching and research of the Italian Baroque, since no such digital archive currently exists.

Work from this project was previously on view in a traveling exhibition with stops in London, Istanbul, Sydney, and Bangalore. This research was also featured as the cover story for The Pennsylvania Gazette.

Earlier in the fall, Saunders participated in a panel that included Mark Robbins, the President of the American Academy in Rome, in celebration of the University of Arkansas's 30th Anniversary of the Rome Center. Saunders is an alumnus of the Fay Jones School of Architecture and Design.

"Baroque Topologies" is part of the Weitzman School's Advanced Research & Innovation Lab (ARI). As part of multi-year plan to provide additional tools and facilities to support the scholarship of faculty and students, ARI opens up vast new territories for innovation and places the School at the forefront of applied and speculative research in several domains.

BRIAN PHILLIPS WINS FIVE AIA AWARDS

Lecturer Brian Phillips's firm Interface Studio Architects (ISA) was recognized by the Philadelphia and Pennsylvania chapters of the American Institute of Architects (AIA) with five Design Awards. Transatlantic, an adaptive reuse project in Philadelphia, was awarded an AIA Philadelphia Gold Medal; Tiny Tower won an AIA Philadelphia Honor Award in the Built

category and an AIA PA Bronze Award; BalletX HQ received an AIA Philadelphia Merit Award for Built Interiors, and Outside-In House was given an AIA PA Bronze Award. Brian Phillips was a Pew Fellow in the Arts in 2011 and the firm was named an Emerging Voice by the Architectural League of New York in 2015.

NOVEMBER 2018

WOMEN IN ARCHITECTURE STUDENTS PRESENT AT HARVARD GSD

Students from Penn Women in Architecture (PWIA) traveled to Cambridge to participate in "A Convergence at the Confluence of Power, Identity and Design" at Harvard's Graduate School of Design on November 3. Master of Architecture students Nicole Bronola, Maria Fuentes, and Caitlin Dashiell presented as one of twelve pecha kucha guest speakers. Their presentation focused PWIA's three pillars of empowerment, exposure, and equity. This included the importance of identity discourse in pedagogy and practice through creation of PWIA firm crawls, a growing mentorship program, and a dialogue between students and practitioners.

KANTER TRITSCH MEDAL AND PRIZE

Alumna Lori Kanter Tritsch (MArch'85) has pledged $1.25 million to establish a $50,000 fellowship for the most promising graduate architecture student at the Stuart Weitzman School of Design and an international medal of excellence for a practicing architect. It is the largest single gift made to the School for fellowships in its 149-year history.

Lori Kanter Tritsch

KANTER TRITSCH MEDAL FOR EXCELLENCE IN ARCHITECTURE
AND ENVIRONMENTAL DESIGN
AWARDED TO ARCHITECTS TOD WILLIAMS AND BILLIE TSIEN
"Tod and Billie have been incredible role models," said Winka Dubbeldam, Miller Professor and Chair in the Department of Architecture. "But more than that, they've been committed to teaching the next generation of architects."

Honored to receive the award, Tsien said, she and Williams were most proud to see a light shining on Penn students whose work focuses on energy, ecology, and social equity.

Williams and Tsien's built projects include the Barnes Foundation (2012), the first major art and education institution in the country to achieve the highest level of environmental certification from the U.S. Green Building Council; and Skirkanich Hall (2006), which houses the School of Engineering and Applied Sciences at Penn. Their firm is currently designing the Obama Presidential Center.

Tod Williams and Billie Tsien

KANTER TRITSCH PRIZE IN ENERGY AND ARCHITECTURAL
INNOVATION AND $50,000 FELLOWSHIP
AWARDED TO 2ND YEAR PENN STUDENT ALEXANDRA MAE ADAMSKI
Calling it a "life-changing" award, Adamski, who will soon enter a field in which women continue to be dramatically underrepresented, said it won't only impact her financial situation, but also her creativity and professional plans upon graduation in May of 2019.

The Prize will be awarded annually to a second-year student pursuing a Master of Architecture degree at the Weitzman School who demonstrates transformational thinking on the built environment and innovation in his or her approach to energy, ecology, and/or social equity.

The Medal and Prize were presented on October 15, 2018 at the IAC Building in New York City as part of the inaugural Weitzman School Awards Ceremony.

Dean Fritz Steiner, Miller Professor and Chair Winka Dubbeldam, MArch Student Alexandra Adamski, and Penn President Amy Gutmann

Alexandra Adamski, Photo by Eddy Marenco

FO
DA
ON

UN
TI

FOUNDATION

by Andrew Saunders, Coordinator

The 501 Architecture Design Studio I project is the product of a semester-long collaboration with the Penn Museum. The Penn Museum is one of the world's great archeology and anthropology research museums, and the largest university museum in the United States. The speculative studio project operates within the ambition of the museum's original masterplan. Only a portion of it was initially built and then halted in 1929. In 1971, the museum began again to expand through numerous additions. The studio project speculates on the Penn Museum as a public interface in the 21st century by designing additional space to accommodate, display and extend the archives that currently house over a million artifacts with only 3% of the collection on display.

The studio begins by analyzing and precisely reconstructing digital and 3D printed models of 3D photogrammetry scanning of original artifacts from the vast museum collection. The process moves beyond the literal representation of the artifacts through a more speculative stage of advanced digital drawing and modeling techniques aimed at interrogating objects, transposing and amplifying specific effects, and opening the objects to architectural interpretation through the generation of novel tectonics and expression.

Building on the concept of space, a group fabrication project consisting of teams of three or four students designed Sequential Chambers for the Curation of Artifacts. The project housed and curate 3D printed replicas of the original vessels each student analyzed in the initial photogrammetry exercise. Each artifact required its own chamber for housing the artifact and at the same time allowing for a calibrated curation of its exhibition. The chambers have relationship to each other as a sequence, but don't necessarily physically connected to one another. The final fabrications were then reinserted in to the context of the Penn Museum as a public exhibition.

The final project of the studio will continue to expand on concepts of space developed in the previous projects. Students develop proposals for the designs of an Archive and Research Extension to the Penn Museum to house research artifacts similar to those analyzed in the initial studio project at the beginning of the semester. The clear set of spatial, material and tectonic principles established in the Sequential Chambers for the Curation of Artifacts exercise evolve in the final project through a full engagement of architectural criteria including, site, context, enclosure, program, circulation, lighting, materiality, space and form.

WITHDRAWN GATEWAY: A NEW ENTRANCE THRESHOLD FOR PENN MUSEUM
Andrew Saunders

CULTURAL NARRATIVES
Cory Henry

Principal of Andrew Saunders Architecture + Design (2004). M.Arch from Harvard GSD with Distinction (2004), B.Arch from Fay Jones School of Architecture, University of Arkansas (1998), Winner of The Robert S. Brown '52 Fellows Program (2013)

Founder of Atelier Cory Henry, Lecturer in Architecture and Design at The University of Southern California, M.Arch from Cornell University School of Architecture, Art and Planning, B.Arch from Drexel University School of Architecture and Media Arts, Research in Design, Cinema and New Media Arts at The Southern California Institute of Architecture (SCIArc)

To begin our collaboration with the Penn Museum and to understand day to day operations of the museum archive, students examined artifacts from excavations around the world. Our section analyzed a cross section of artifacts from the late English archaeologist C. Leonard Woolley and his disciples. Many of the artifacts had been buried deep in the oldest section of archives dating back to opening of the museum in 1899. The artifacts were cataloged but had rarely been exhibited or viewed since their excavation.

Upon retrieval of the artifacts, museum archivists discovered never before published turn of the century documentation from the excavation. The descriptive drawing technique followed conventions of Eugene Jahnke (1863-1921) and Fritz Emde's (1873-1951) *Tables of Functions with Formulae and Curves* (German: *Funktionentafeln Mit Formeln und Kurven*), a landmark of the visual presentation of complex surfaces published in 1909 (shortly before the excavations).

A series of three analytical drawings were made for each artifact. Each drawing documents a specific boundary region of the dig where the artifact was discovered. The convention at the time was to parcel the dig site into distinct regions based on a Cairo grid module. The artifact was positioned in the Cairo module documenting its orientation with the ground when excavated.

The analytical procedures contained within these drawings generated spatial, geometric and material consequences setting the underlaying foundation for the final proposals for the extension of the Penn Museum archives.

This studio investigated the ability of architecture to articulate culture, define place, and negotiate territories through the manipulation of space. To accomplish this, students worked on a series of projects focused on the University of Pennsylvania Museum of Archaeology and Anthropology. They investigated these ideas through object, form, and space making in three related projects.

In the first project, students designed a container for an artifact focusing on the idea of collection and preservation. In the second project, they developed a pavilion to present curated and contained objects. The third project was a design for a new exhibition space located in the existing courtyard of the museum. The final project required students to look across scales from the site to the surrounding neighborhood, understanding their project as a container, object, and place marker.

Architecture is often viewed as an entity or object, rather than an "event" or "space" of social and political relations. Conceptually, students were challenged to critique power structures, inequalities historically present in western museum collection practices. This was done to reveal the politics and social production of space as a means to generate architectural propositions in contrapposto to existing practices. Mediums such as narrative and image were used to tell specific stories of territory, identity, politics, culture, and time. Therefore, each project is engendered from a contextual social commentary rather than aesthetic or fetishized pursuit.

COLLAGE GROUND SPACE
K Brandt Knapp

READING MIS-READING
Daniel Markiewicz

Co-founder of BRANDT:HAFERD, Winner of the inaugural FOLLY competition (2012), Teaches at Weitzman School, Columbia's GSAPP, NJIT, Pratt & Barnard, M.Arch from Yale School of Architecture (2010), B.S.D & B.A. from Arizona State University (2006)

Lecturer, Partner of FORMA Architects PLLC, Co-Editor of the architecture journal: PROJECT, Partner of Aether Images, Formally an Associate at Diller Scofidio + Renfro, M.Arch from the Yale School of Architecture, B.S.E. in Civil Engineering/ Architecture from Princeton University

Our approach to the Museum Extension / Archive project built upon the studio at large syllabus and the workshop with Sir Peter Cook, which emphasized a study of SPACE. We worked iteratively under two investigation titles: *Grounding Collage: Serial Studies* and *Archive Happenings: Constructed Environments*. Each student was to understand / define SPACE by first looking to *what ground is*, as it relates to techniques of collage. Abstract concepts were studied by articulating boundary, territory, surface and joining techniques through drawings and physical "collage models." Spatializing in three dimensions how these collage pieces come together producing various conditions, allowed for an evaluation of space and sequence that contributed to the narrative development. *What is the role of the archive today* was the underlying question when envisioning the "happenings" that take place through time in the proposals.

The sequence of happenings were to be developed and worked through the plan organization of the architecture, building a narrative that unified the conceptual underpinnings, formal / material studies of the collage models, and the story of what an archive is today. The studios emphasis on the ground and the relationship between building and intervention, made for an emphasis on section as well. The results of the studio were diverse and collage proved to be conceptually rich, manifesting in various different ways—programmatic, built structure, material and/or environmental.

The purpose of this studio was to design an Archive extension of the Penn Museum. From the beginning students were asked to question how they read and represent architecture through drawing. Issues of perception, perspective, and distortion arose during early stage assignments that focused on the act of intentionally and productively mis-reading architectural drawings in order to produce new three dimensional form. These spatial tricks translated into a diverse array of formal languages that were then deployed through the design of the archive extension. The studio asked students to develop their own approach to the archive based on their early studies, essentially to formulate their own set of questions and then defend that rigorously through design. Some questions that were raised over the course of the studios' explorations included but were not limited to: Can the design and production of uninhabitable monuments critique the methods of display currently used by the Penn Museum? Can the circuitous and confined nature of a maze reflect the inner workings of typically concealed and hermetic archival operations? Can the form of an architectural extension mirror the Penn Museum's physically constrained site and their limited options for expansion?

Regardless of students' initial investigation each project had to address core issues related to the design of an Archive Extension of the Penn Museum including: Site Strategies within a complex existing courtyard, Programmatic relationships, Circulation between existing and proposed museum spaces, Security and the interface between Public and Private zones of activity, Entry and Facade. Students were asked to develop their ideas through Plan, Section, Perspective and Model. Color was excluded from consideration to allow students to focus on the basics of architecture.

PROTOMORPHS: EMERGENT ONTOLOGICAL FORMATIONS
Danielle Willems

Co-Founder of Mæta Design (2008). Visiting Professor at the Pratt Institute. M.Arch from Columbia University, GSAPP (2007)

Protomorphs' perceives the architectural production as part of a larger, self-organizing, material process. While engaging in the production of proto-morphic-architectural environments through the generative capacities of algorithmic /diagrammatic logics, our primary focus will be the relationship between city and architecture. Finding the constitutive difference between the two in time, more so than in form. Protomorph is an investigation into the processes of becoming, and as such, it fuses the two modes of thought into a unified phase space. One of the challenges in the studio will be the re-invention of the means of assessment, the development of notations, and techniques that will document the forces and the production of "difference" in the spatial manifestations of the generative systems. With the introduction of a secondary scale of time in the design process, borrowing a concept from biology, symbiogenesis will be the primary force in the evolution of the projects.

The studio methodology consists of three feedback layers: generative diagram, prototyping model, and video. The generative diagram is the assembly machine to forms. The physical model should be a method of rapid prototyping the limits of the generative diagram in order to make specific spaces/scapes and formal behaviors in relationship to the projects spatial/temporal thesis.

The video component will be used as a different method of exploring, experimenting, generating spatial sequences, creating immersive environments, and building a narrative inside or through the architectural forms.

WITHDRAWN GATEWAY
Andrew Saunders

CRITIC: ANDREW SAUNDERS

Paul Germaine McCoy

Legend

...every surface telling a story about their origins, every edge and crack reminding us of the journey that has brought it to this precious and fragile state. If these artifacts hold such importance to our culture, then the new archive should demand that our culture contemplates the privilege of accessing them in a special, restricted, and controlled space.

Xinyi Huang

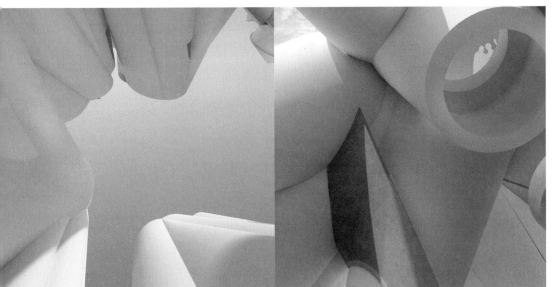

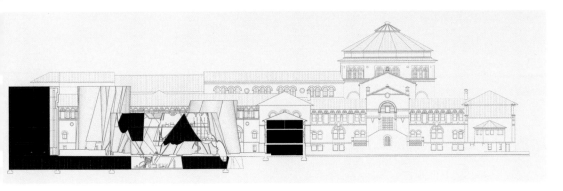

Cones are used to create these surfaces, serving as the display space and the opening to other levels. When cones extend, they become surfaces that separate the project from the courtyard. When cones penetrate the floors, they allow light come into interior and public can peek into the private archive spaces.

Alan Fan

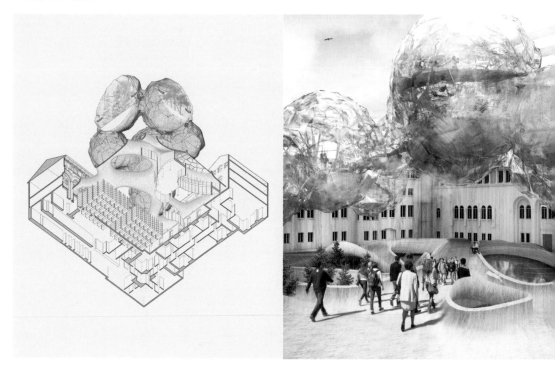

Each bubble will have its own climate, exhibiting cultural artifacts in their own environment. Middle Eastern artifacts would be housed in an arid desert habitat as Inuit cultural items shall be placed in a tundra. One will notice another park beneath them, parks in both sky and ground. Either being above or below, one will have a feeling of being in a new fantastical world.

Megan York

The archives embraces the two forces of the natural & the artificial, through a symbiotic relationship. Computer servers and databases create the core with its intricate surfaces that are able to input & output information in relation to the archives & programmatic space. The cavernous form, is dictated by the intricacies & power of the new archival technologies.

Merrick Castillo

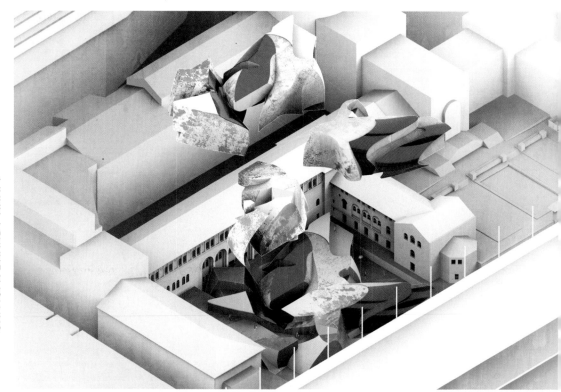

Plant life takes on a new life & begins to take over the archive, allowing for the natural inhabitants to become viewers of the archive. Creating new microclimates within the addition for plant life & animal life to view the artifacts...As people enter they are faced with a surreal landscape, giving the high ground to the artifacts & natural landscape making the human the object on display.

COLLAGE GROUND SPACE
K Brandt Knapp

Maria Jose Fuentes

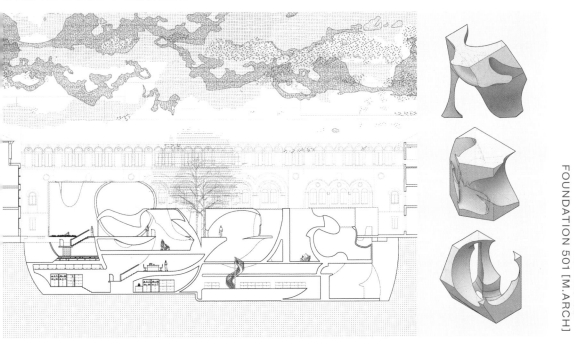

Meandering forms are reformulated by the modular component which create a categorical map of essences that can be picked & probed to create an enigmatic circulation. Three components of modularization were used to crate the forms which shift from macro to micro scale through levels of degree & kind; which have been sifted through a filter of materiality & light conditions.

Yi-Hsuan Wu

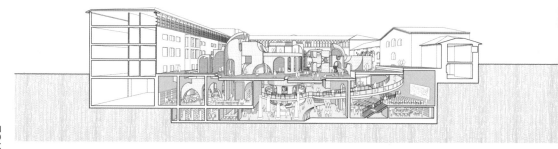

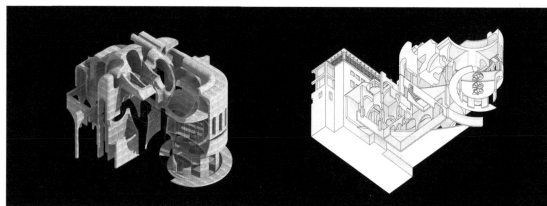

The high arches resonate the murmurs of the artifacts, they listen and absorb the secrets. This place is like a tomb, but also a rebirth; it's a place of shackle, but then a place of sanctuary. Every turn and moment exudes different narratives, low mutterings from artifacts escape normal detection, but the form of them tells the story.

Daniel Markiewicz

Peik Shelton

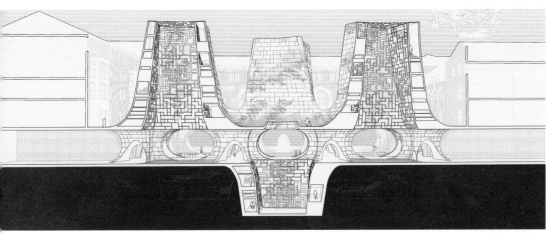

From the exterior, a hulking presence is demanded in the courtyard but an ephemeral skin allows viewers on the street level just a glimpse of the intricacies that lie witthin in hopes of evoking curiosity and adventure. The extension's interior then provides visitors and researchers different ways in which to orient themselves around the collection of artifacts.

PROTOMORPHS: EMERGENT ONTOLOGICAL FORMATIONS
Danielle Willems

Matt Kohman

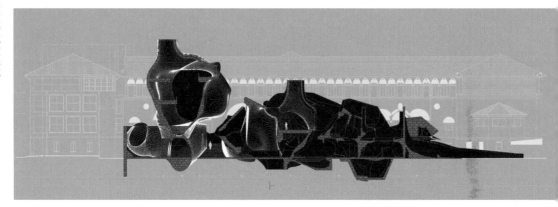

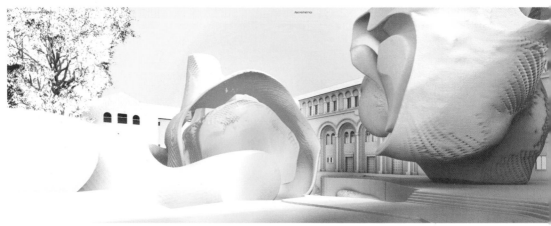

As manifested in this proposal, figures nest and penetrate a new submerged ground plane where existing conditions maintain hierarchical control over circulation, forcing travel underneath rather than through an existing gate, as an example. Within the museum typology this moves towards a deeper reading of the museum object and its contents.

Yang Zhenxiong

The polychromed surfaces can be seemed as the ornamentation but more as the process of the cultural collection. Within this contained space, antiques' identity has been integrated into the museum through the reflection, refraction, and transparency. Therefore, the change of antiques also brought the new identity to the museum.

SEPTEMBER 5TH, 2018
DREAMS - REALITIES - EXPLORATIONS
Sir Peter Cook

CRAB installation: *Towards Comfo-Veg*, Los Angeles, 2012.

SEPTEMBER 12TH, 2018
BOTH, AND
Dream The Combine
Tom Carruthers and Jennifer Newsom

Clearing in Shafer, MN, 2017

SEPTEMBER 17TH, 2018
ALPHAVILLE, THE CITY LAYER,
AND THE NEW NORMAL
Benjamin H. Bratton

The Stack: On Software and Sovereignty, MIT Press, 2016

Dispute Plan to Prevent Future Luxury Constitution,
e-flux journal series with Sternberg Press, 2015

ennDesign

THE STATE OF WATER
Winka Dubbeldam, Matthijs Bouw, Almut Gruntuch Ernst, Anna Kostreva

Workshop Collaboration with TU Braunschweig and ANCB [AEDES] Berlin, Spring 2019, Funded by DAAD via TU Braunschweig

Political dynamics, climate change and demographic changes are contemporary global challenges. In our research-based teaching, we rely on a holistic methodology and an inter-culturally engaged design network to bring about future-oriented architectural answers to worldwide issues.

The 2019 collaborative workshop will specifically focus on global ecological challenges concerning architecture and water. Themes like climate change, politics, and infrastructure, will form the lenses to understand contemporary cities in the context of a transforming environment. Flooding, drought and other forms of extreme weather are observed more and more as normal occurrences everywhere on the planet. The impact of urbanization, its global reaches into rural, oceanic, and atmospheric environments, has become immense. Human impact thus forms an ongoing feedback loop of dynamic interactions between the built and non-built environment.

The river environments of the Spree and the Mississipi are two focus areas identified for the projects of the workshop. The long-term interactions between humans and water along rivers will be analyzed and discussed as catchment areas for ecological, technological, industrial and social realities. Topics of spatio-temporal transformations like mobility, pollution, and resource extraction will be looked at as water culture that is both human and non-human in order to inform future-oriented design projects.

Thus, the workshop will engage with these topics in active design research. Students will prepare presentations before their arrival on the context and thematic content of their project interest. During the workshop week, design projects will be brainstormed and developed in groups and partner work.

The main teaching goal of the workshop is to support student projects dealing with complex global themes, done in an intensive week-long collaborative workshop environment. The architectural projects should reach a level of rigorous complexity with thorough programming. The students are thus challenged to grasp the design question and its implications in order to clarify it analytically. Then, they formulate a conceptual idea as a solution. The experimental and methodological processes develops into an architectural design with a subject-specific focus. Students engage in finding architectural solutions through the design process and in clearly communicating and discussing their ideas. Throughout, the students will be consistently accompanied in their projects by individual and group tutorials with assistant professors as well as presentations with the lead professors.

Additional informative input will come from invited lectures and excursions into Berlin's history and interaction between water and architecture, for example, including visits to municipal brick water towers, the Ludwig Leo Bau (Versuchsanstalt für Wasserbau und Schiffbau), the Ökohaus by Frei Otto, the proposed Flussbad site, as well as a city history tour about the Spree and Berlin's canals. Students will also participate in the ongoing Anthropocene Curriculum at the Haus der Kultur der Welt, which currently has a research project on the Mississippi River. The workshop will end with formal presentations with an invited jury and a reflective discussion about the experimental work done during the week.

Instructors:
Winka Dubbeldam, Miller Professor and Chair of Architecture
Matthijs Bouw, Professor of Practice in Resilience
TA: Ryan Barnette
Almut Gruntuch Ernst, Professor, TU Braunschweig
TA: Anna Kostreva

FOUNDATION
by Annette Fierro, Coordinator

Devoted to the theme of architecture in and of the city, our first task in ARCH 502 is to acquaint ourselves with a slice of the great literature of the city, and ends in proposing a building which reflects upon and incorporates some of these ideas. Here an understanding of "site" is one which reflects local and regional contingencies in all of their complexities, as a well as an expanded relationship with "construct," developing an understanding of urbanism which is informed by disciplinary foregrounding. ARCH 502 this year takes as its critical framework a re-examination of the early writings of Aldo Rossi, whose seminal influence on the development of post-modernism in the 1960s was based in his reaction to the scientific urbanism inherent in the modernist city. His writings on the claim of architecture to its own "autonomy," proposed in the prominence of functionalist analysis, has continuing relevance in the resurgence of this term in current debate. Rossi proposed that the city might be regarded as a collection of urban artifacts, each with their own knowledge and memory, themselves subject to complex political, economic, and sociological forces, or as he puts it, "social content:" the city (and its history) was a "skeleton," an organizer of memories and residues. The totality of the city was far more important than a separate reading of pieces and parts. Our task in ARCH 502 is to investigate these ideas once again, but in using different tools of representations to address very contemporary issues, re-invigorate seminal terms: memory, autonomy, and typology.

The project for this semester is an urban market, a fundamental typology of urban building, historically functioning as the *agora*, the center of social and civic life. While urban markets still function in this capacity to varying degrees around the world, the urban market in the United States can be traced through a series of diminishments. Our market exists in this point of re-examination, particularly in the challenge that different forms of online exchange and different economic conditions have wrought on tangible commercial settings. Our site is on the periphery of Manayunk, originally an industrial mill town on the banks of the Schuylkill, which was eventually incorporated within Philadelphia's municipal boundaries. Artifacts of this industrial past vary from major forms of infrastructure which border and contain our specific site, as well as mill buildings themselves which have been abandoned and repurposed through different historical pasts. The development of an adjacent main street has considerably contributed to the gentrification of the surrounding areas, a situation in which our site, on the edge of this development, is explicitly implicated.

EMBEDDED CHARACTERS
Annette Fierro

NONCONFORM
Maya Alam

M.Arch from Rice University (1984), B.S. in Civil Engineering from Rice University (1980), Author of *The Glass State: The Technology of the Spectacle, Paris, 1981-1998* (MIT Press, 2003)

Co-Founder of Alam / Profeta, US | IT | DE, 2016/17 inaugural Harry der Boghosian Fellow, M.Arch from SCI-Arc, Los Angeles, Dipl. Ing. from Peter Behrens School o Architecture, Düsseldorf

"Typological form refers, then, to a form, which, either as a result of its being chosen during certain periods or the implications ascribed to it, has ended up assuming the specific character of a process which exactly manifests the form itself." (Aldo Rossi, *Architecture of the City*)

The question of typologies is one which has defined, challenged and beleaguered architecture. Could there ever be static, singly defined set of elements which comprise ever-changing cities? If a typology, in Rossi's terms, synopsizes a universal condition which is cultural, climatological, even political—what in the typology redefines itself within its architectural language? With how much latitude can these be both defined and re-written and with what kinds of criteria? Does architectural form even have the capacity to reflect a highly complex multivalent contextual setting? In redefining what a typology is and is not, and why it is relevant, this studio incorporates multiple sets of aspects and events, and speculates how they can become embedded within form. We incorporate specifically scenarios and narratives around the multiple functions of an urban market, engaging architectural elements of interface as the setting for re-examining actions of exchange, barter, sale, and trade. We observe and notate conditions of exchange as they exist now. We write and deploy narrative scripts which will embed the site's historical aspects and contemporary preoccupations, organized by categories and characteristics, into the architecture of the market. We collect and categorize, transform and translate, iterate and combine.

We operate through categories, norms, filters and standards to feel connected and to communicate sufficiently with others. However, such an ingrained mode of classification also makes us vulnerable to error, reluctant to change, and ignorant to the "other." Today, to partake in the ever-growing complexity of our cultural landscapes, it is paramount to cultivate a space of engagement across multiple views of the world. Our audience today extends to include machines, and the biases we maintain when dealing with each other permeate the hard- and softwares we create: in fact, too often we end up confusing such automatized processes as being neutral. One of the most infamous examples is the case of the Kodak Shirley Cards that created a fair skin bias in 20th-century photography. This phenomenon is still permeating our understanding of photos and images today, and the fact that it went unchallenged for so long is one of the evidences that technology is often taken for granted as based on science, and therefore incontestable.

Comparably, our site investigation will look critically at surveying technology, its data biases, what we understand as real and true. Who controls what we see and how we see it? What is included in our digital (Google) earth but also, maybe more importantly, what is not.

We looked closely at the phenomenon of Silicon Valley start-ups, like *Imperfect Produce* and its Philadelphia equivalent *Misfits Market*, that understood the interrelationship between our aesthetic ideals and waste culture by selling perfectly good produce that would otherwise be trashed because it does not conform to the market's norms.

In place of the online format that these new markets propose, we will envision a local, cyclical model that counters waste culture in more than one way. The reuse of compost, clothes, electronics, etc. was closely studied and incorporated in the Market's program.

SPOLIA REDUX
Brian De Luna

DIFFERENTIATED REDUNDANCIES
Joshua Freese

MS. AAD. Columbia University, 2009, B.Arch. Southern California Institute of Architecture 2006

B.Design in Architectural Studies from Florida International University, M.Arch from PennDesign, Founder of Archifreese (Freese LLC), 2017

Cities, from the unbuilt/theoretical to the existing/developing, are extensive systems that reflect and record histories and memories, one that goes beyond the contextual framework of the built environment. Understanding and cataloging cities into a myriad of different architectural typologies, one can begin to define the built environment as a series of "artifacts" and "memories" that also retain and record hidden characteristics and less tangible histories.

This Studio will begin with multiple modes of researching and cataloging city "memories" and "artifacts" through graphic and symbolic representation. The first exercises will study cartography, texture, data, projection, and topographic types of mapping. We will research and explore how to layer different, various elements and results of the cultural, social, topographic and the built environment. The market will be a culmination and hybridization of the multiple exercises from 2D and 3D objects and graphics. We will also use a selected architecture precedent "Artifact" and a conceptual theme from Aldo Rossi to produce a stereometric Euclidian object that should inform the spatial and programmatic embodiment of the proposed market. This Studio will include historic precedents from the Baroque to the Contemporary.

The market is one of the most ancient and prevalent of architectural typologies and a collective model of differentiated redundancies. Architecturally and programmatically it is designed for different people, programs, and sites, constructed using different forms, materials and techniques. It is usually redundant in general terms of categorical content and architectural or structural typology (shed/span/gridded hall). New markets have emerged which take on the original features of the market; fluctuating in content, internal organization, mobility, and permanence They also challenge the content and role of the market in a city and are focusing on cultural value, social space, and the spectacle of daily life.

Manayunk is also a collection of differentiated redundancies. The dimensional and general aesthetic redundancy of the rowhouses ascending the hills are given their differentiated characteristics through the different finishes, furnishings and decorations applied by the residents. The once thriving mills and factories are differentiated in terms of their original content, current use and refurbishments, but they have a series of typological redundancies in terms of structure, construction, material, and form.

Design differentiation and individual projects will be created by each student using and assembling prescriptive and redundant references, site and programmatic constraints, technical methods, and representational typologies. Students will need to clearly define their response to the contemporary market as an architectural, spatial and structural typology. Students will also need to define ambitions and intent for their design strategy in specific regards to the value and consequences, both necessary and ideal, of the content, forms, and features of a marketplace on this specific site in the city.

MISCELLANY
Andrew Lucia

ARCHITECTURE'S POLITICAL AUTONOMY: COMMONING MANAYUNK
Eduardo Rega

Founding Principal of LUCITO (www.lucito.co), Andrew Lucia (Solo Art Practice, www. andrewlucia.com), 2015-17 Cass Gilbert Visiting Fellow, University of Minnesota, University of Pennsylvania, M.Arch, 2008, University of Minnesota, B.A. in Architecture, 2001

Founder of Architectures of Refusal, Editor in *urbanNext*, Actar publishers, M.Sc. in Advanced Architectural Design from Columbia University, GSAPP, M.Arch from Polytechnic University of Madrid, ETSAM, B.Arch from University of Las Palmas de Gran Canaria ·

This studio section approaches the city and typology of the market as objects comprising vast repositories of distributed elements through time, clouds of particles and points that aggregate massive collections of material, data and memories. A point, by definition, is dimensionless, having no further qualities assigned to its being save a location in space and time. Considered in this manner, the urban condition and market can be seen as a massive skeletal cloud whose attributes, inhabitants, values, desires, qualities, and memories are continually ascribed and exchanged on an evolving basis. And yet in both of these types, residues of the past persist as artifacts, echoes whose permanence give rise to an overarching sense of identity and character.

The image, as a medium of exchange, will also play a critical role in this studio. As a society now primarily mediated via the image, we are arguably in a process of transition from one governed by a regime of orthographic geometric protocols to one comprised of vast distributions of information and spatial data.

Approached as a question of fidelity of measurement or experience, when zooming in to either a material urban condition or a quantized image, mid-scale boundaries give way to hazy densities of microelements whose figures are only revealed when observed at the macro level. Yet the urban condition, much like the traditional image, has been subject to procedures that collapse potentially complex spatial and material conditions to one of planar projection, shape, and figure. An image read similarly would be regarded as a caricature, reduced to gross boundaries and having lost tremendous amounts of information through processes of oversimplification. The actual condition in both cases is far more nuanced and complex, not reflective of their lived experiences that are rich, aggregate and irreducible.

In an attempt to offer an alternative to the game, Monopoly, Commonspoly was recently released to illuminate, through play, alternative non-exploitative processes of city-making. For its capacity to broadly educate on the general dynamics of urban development by questioning current regimes of property, our studio aimed to redesign the Commonspoly board game to reflect the specificities of Manayunk. This served as a launchpad for our critical discussions around architecture's entanglement in the systems of power that produce the city. Through the act of playing, and generating various scenarios, we explored systems of exchange and forms of ownership, where profit is replaced by benefit, market value by use value, and where accumulations of capital and private property are challenged by the collective reclamation of the commons.

Our syllabus took the Market as a Giant House as its main program. In its origins, the market was also the Agora, the center of political life in the city. In Commonspoly, like in occupy movements and popular revolutions across the world, the Agora is also the space where a collective uprising against state and corporate domination can be staged. Our studio would therefore treat the market as an Agora, a typology where principles of distribution, cooperation and access prioritize public benefit and oppose private profit maximization. Critically engaging with the Market's open and expanded functions as a Giant House we studied its potential as the organizational center of Manayunk's commons: an urban political activator, an open cooperative, a micro-factory, an urban community garden, etc. Our expanded Market-as-Agora would be both a platform for, and a trigger of alternative modes of governance, ownership and local economic development that can support the neighborhood in resisting the threatening wave of gentrification.

URBAN RELIEF: MARKETPLACE FOR MANAYUNK
Andrew Saunders

Principal of Andrew Saunders
Architecture + Design (2004).
M.Arch from Harvard GSD with
Distinction (2004), B.Arch from
Fay Jones School of Architecture,
University of Arkansas (1998),
Winner of The Robert S. Brown
'52 Fellows Program (2013)

A charge of the 502 semester will be to take on the legacy of Aldo Rossi through his major work of architectural and urban theory, *The Architecture of the City*. To begin, the studio constructs reliefs based on both existing and archeological urban artifacts from the Manayunk neighborhood of Philadelphia. Parallel analysis of Louise Nevelson's assemblages will inform formal and compositional conditions of framing, grid, edge, figure, ground, light, shadow and Euclidean figuration. The studio will explore the flexibility and discrete conditions of Nevelson's assemblages, her arrangements and how they are motivated by interpretations of Mondrian grid compositions. By slowing down perception and making "strange" the familiar, a refreshing perception renews the familiar and draws attention to the artistic procedures operating on it. Building on the Manayunk Reliefs in the initial exercise, the studio becomes immersed in the material culture and context of Manayunk, both existing and archeological.

With increasing interest in reviving the fortunes of struggling communities, older industrial cities represent promising regions for strategic investment and critical centers for promoting inclusive economic growth. The project of 502 will be an urban market. The program of the market will be defined individually by each students—a market for what? With a rich history of turn of the century booming industry, the studio will pose the question of what new industries could spark social and economical growth in Manayunk in the 21st century? Through an entrepreneurial approach, each student will research and propose a contemporary program for the market. The entrepreneurial programs draw from both traditional guilds of Philadelphia as well as emerging models of industry. Each specific program will begin to inform the nature of the new urban market, fostering a new typology of unexpected exchange with the community.

EMBEDDED CHARACTERS
Annette Fierro

Alexander N. Brown

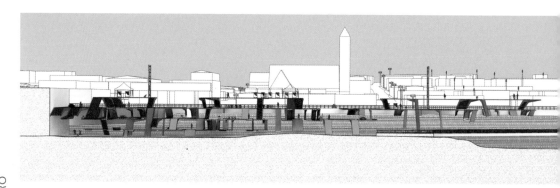

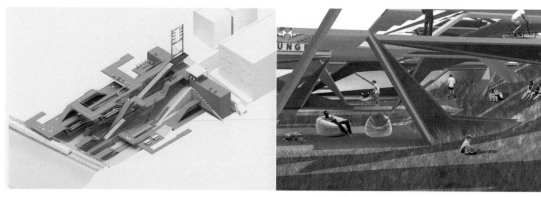

The platforms are to look almost continuous as they flow between elevation heights of the site, generating floors, walls, and roof systems. The fluctuation between structural systems begin to describe a density that is found in the city of Manayunk itself, through its buildings, infrastructure, and topography changes. Here in the market, circulation alter the levels of transparency.

Sami Samawi

Consumers can request products and are now active participants in their
fruition. This new platform is one where ideas are exchanged and where
the brainstorming happens with both the users and the makers to create
superior products embedded with narrative that respond exactly to the
consumer's needs.

NONCONFORM
Maya Alam

Michael Niklas Caine

CRITIC: MAYA ALAM

The collection of twisted blocks creates a series of interior nodes that serve as an added vertical landscape, acting as flexible space for mini-markets, festivals and performances. While the massing of the market acts as a large, cavernous place with interspersed floor slabs, upon entering the building, it reveals itself as a continuous tunnel with impromptu viewing platforms.

Maria Fuentes

...ats of dye are on display, showcasing the waste of both water and color
...eturning to where it can be repurposed to create more than what we
...oss into the trash. Here, one can embrace a queerness that moves towards
...binary fusion of non-normality that weaves into the gentrification of
...he growing town.

Natalia Revelo La Rotta

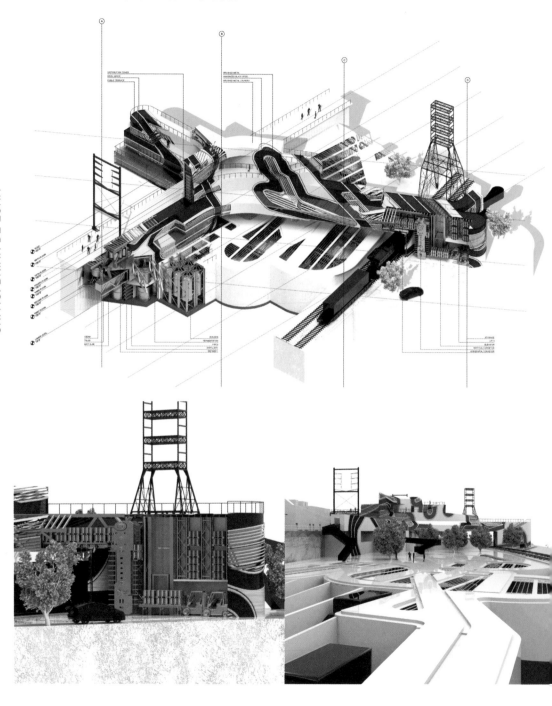

As an alley of networks, the building takes the city grid on a deconstructive path through its construction. These typologies run from large scale to small scale, distilling and filtering its participants as the space constricts. Similar to a city street system, the building acts as a system for filtering large raw resources.

SPOLIA REDUX
rian De Luna

Robert Schaffer

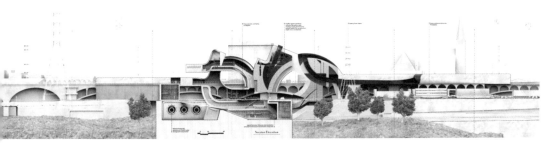

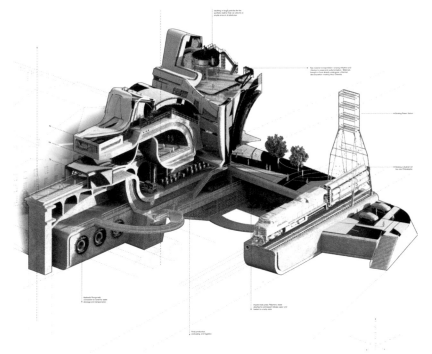

Isometric Cutaway

rawing inspiration from Renaissance architecture and the leather markets
at were created there, the new proposed project is a synthetic leather
arket, combining memories of the cities booming textile industry while
ilizing the river that rests on the sites border. The proposal consumes
e once pedestrian bridge, creating a public space that moves through.

Qiao Yu

The faceted spaces were assigned to maximize the use efficiency as well as balance the complexity of the forms and geometry of the other programs. Patterns were used on the interior to create distractions when there were changes in program, scale of space, or profile of the space, in order to create a smooth transition as people move between different environments.

DIFFERENTIATED REDUNDANCIES
Joshua Freese

Molly Zmich

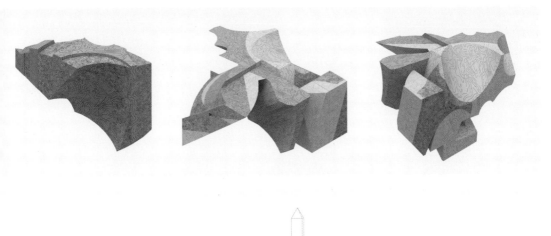

The ornamental geometric facade creates a false nature where vegetation typically occurs, real plant growth occurs on the interior of the building inside of ornamental volumes, creating an inversion of reality. This play on perception and scale also takes place in the patterning and manipulation of repeating geometries at various scales throughout the building.

MISCELLANY
Andrew Lucia

CRITIC: ANDREW LUCIA

Yang Zhenxiong

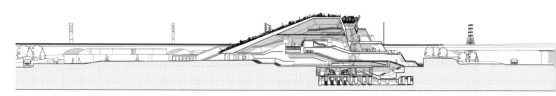

To provide further understanding of the transformation between the quantity of manufactured product and the quality of nature environment, the process of e-waste recycling has been exposed to the visitors as the primary purpose of the market.

Rachael L. Kulish

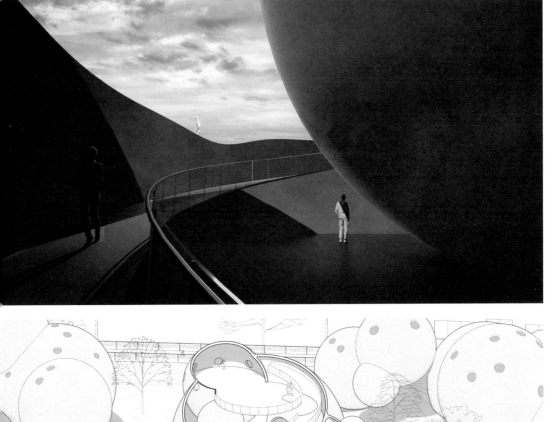

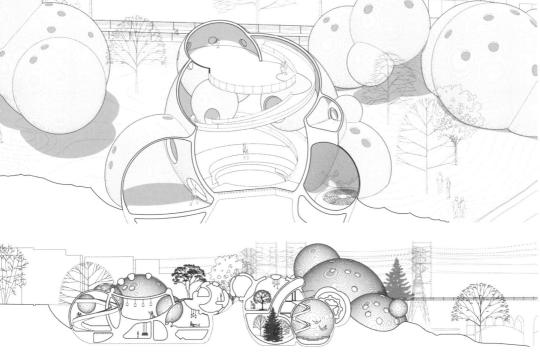

Relationships between boundary collections were drawn through a set of rules to both disrupt, co-exist, and dominate the manifesting boundaries, revealing qualities that challenge biases and unveil opportunities. The market's main commodity, air, as an entity that organizes space through diametric placement in order to blend spaces of both contained and uncontained.

Qiyuan Cao

CRITIC: EDUARDO REGA

WE ARE IN THE
ENDGAME NOW

Building components are easy to deploy and to manufacture in very narrow
structures that liberate the urban space around them. Based on people's
and organization's demand, building components can be customized and distributed. An extention of the Philadelphia Area Cooperative Alliance network
in which exchange of services are based on solidarity and not competition.

Veronica Rosado

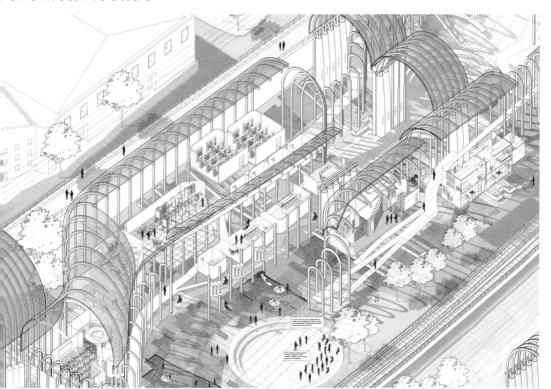

20-year spatial proposal for alternative non-exploitative and anti-author-arian models of development, ownership and governance as they produce the built environment. It is aim to spatialize these through an implementation divided into 3 phases: Demonstration Expo, Productive Protocols Integration, and Hyperdecentralized Expansions.

Kyunghyun Kim

The solid, heavy-looking steel structures with green paint is reinterpreted into light and transparent mesh with matt green color. The visual density of mesh varies from the point of views and the visual variety gives freshness of the place to visitors. Specifically, the shapes of urban artifacts overlap because of the transparency of the mesh.

Andrew Saunders

Peik Shelton

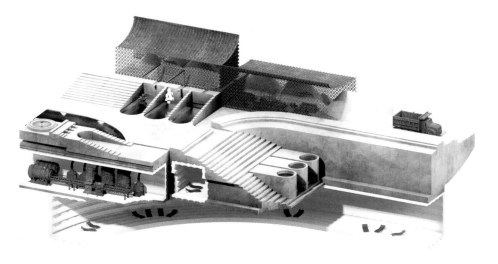

With the advent of Amazon and online marketplaces, the Saline Royale seeks to return to the aspects of a market that have begun to be lost in 21st century. Its an estranged and experiential urbanity in itself that returns to notions of community and spectacle as it is fitted with salted meat vendors, salt storage for the city, salt therapy caves, spas, and salt sculpture gardens.

GALLERY

Megan York
Critic: Maya Alam

Qiao Yu
Critic: Josh Freese

Yi-Hsuan Wu
Critic: Annette Fierro

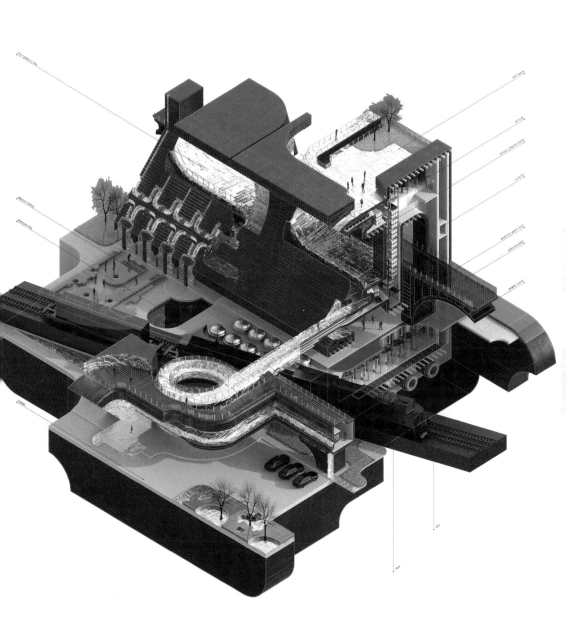

Eddy Sheng
Critic: Brian De Luna

Merrick Castillo
Critic: K Brandt Knapp

Kyunghyun Kim
Critic: Andrew Saunders

CO

CORE
by Hina Jamelle, Coordinator

The Core 601 Urban Housing Studios define new contemporary modes of living in an urban environment. In a world of increasing demand on existing resources there is newly focused attention on adaptive reuse and the expansion of existing facilities. Each Urban Housing studio section will position the housing project relative to an existing structure. The student proposals will be required to engage with this existing building condition—with 1/3 of the proposed project interacting directly with the existing structure while the remaining 2/3 to be new construction. A goal is to encourage the production of hybrid forms, programs and architectural conditions that interrogate relationships between new and existing conditions.

All Studio Sections develop housing projects of 50,000 sq ft. on an Urban Lot with a minimum of two facades. The housing project is designed as a hybrid form of housing/dwelling which includes a commercial or cultural program that can co-exist with housing. Other key objectives include the study of a buildings massing and the physical impact it makes on the city with a highly detailed façade.

The use of digital techniques is a given for this semester's projects, but the goal is to use these technologies in an opportunistic fashion for the generation of growth and the evaluation of patterns in the development of the overall form. In particular, each studio examines part-to-whole organizations and their potential for architecture by offering the tools to create effects that exceed the sum of their parts.

Most part-to-whole organizations share common characteristics, including structure: defined by parts and their composition; and the interconnectivity of the various parts that have functional, structural, and spatial relationships with each other. During this semester, a primacy is given to formations that are varied, accumulative, and subject to change that may shift spatial experiences, scale, and material aspects. In addition, buildings are to incorporate program, spatiality, structure, and enclosure into a singular formation that incorporates a range of experiences and formal variations of gradated intensities and patterns.

The form of the building impacts the selected urban environment. Each instructor provides their own site within a city of the instructor's choice. As a building contributes to the city in which the building is located-each individual studio's methodology involves assignments that develop relationships between building plans, sections and façade— together with an understanding of vertical and horizontal pedestrian circulation.

Across all studio's there are two separate event weeks: Plan week immediately precedes the Mid Review and addresses unit design, clear divisions of public and private spaces, building circulation and preliminary documentation of life safety, egress and ADA requirements. The Section and Façade Week immediately follows the Mid Review and addresses an understanding of vertical and horizontal circulation, building program distribution, façade design and documentation.

SHIFTING HYBRIDS: ADAPTIVE REUSE ON THE LOWER EAST SIDE OF NYC
Hina Jamelle

MEGA-BLOCK REDUX III
Kutan Ayata

Architect and Director, Contemporary Architecture Practice, New York (2002) and Shanghai (2014), Awarded Fifty Under Fifty: Innovators of the 21st Century (2015), Awarded Architectural Record Design Vanguard Award (2004), Author: Elegance. Architectural Design, John Wiley and Sons Inc., London. (2007)

Co-Founded Young & Ayata (2008) Awarded Architectural League Prize (2014), M.Arch from Princeton University (2004), BFA in Architecture fr Massachusetts College of Art i Boston (1999)

This studio will examine emergence and its relation to the formulation of architecture by using digital techniques in an opportunistic fashion for the generation of growth and evaluation of patterns in the development of form. In particular, this studio will examine part to whole organizations and its potential for architecture by offering the tools to create effects that exceed the sum of their parts.

The program for the studio is a new residential building on the site of the Sunshine Theater, located on the Lower East Side in downtown Manhattan. The student proposals will be required to engage with this existing building condition—with 1/3 of the proposed project interacting directly with the Sunshine Theater while the remaining 2/3 to be new construction. Our Studio will be joined at key junctures by Martha Kelley from Goldman Sachs. Her division the Real Estate Principal Investment Area [REPIA] makes direct, opportunistic equity and credit investments in real estate assets and portfolios around the country. Each student will refine the particular program and strategy for the new business model during the course of the semester. The goal for each student is to deal with a range of familiar architectural issues- how to turn a corner, multi-room configurations and circulation patterns for example. The intended result is a project exhibiting innovative architectural organizations and strategies for market and affordable housing using topological surfaces, unit arrangements and patterns scaling from an individual room to the entire building with different spatial and material qualities contributing to the development of architecture.

One of the most significant impacts of 20th Centu modernist urbanism discourse was the implementation of mega-blocks. Mega-Blocks can b described as top-down interventions as over-sized urban blocks, typically containing a homogeneo architectural character enabling large scale interventions, originally for social housing ambition within growing urban areas through the means of welfare state. The studio, over the course of thr years, worked collectively to speculate on Stuyvesant Town, an 18-block territory in New Yo City, and imagined alternative future scenarios for the next 20 years. We fully embraced the pe manence of the physical context, the good, the bad, the ugly, and accepted all that it has as a 3-dimensional site to operate on. What is there remained there to initiate the next stage of urba development. We added, subtracted, intersected fused, gutted, grew, bridged the existing typolo to produce new masses, new characters. Each student generated a proposal in a specific cour yard or the building of the complex with their self-generated mix programmed housing agenda create a heterogeneous urbanity. The collective effort of the studio aspired to transform the sel similar spatial and homogeneous urban character towards distinct moments of difference within t complex. The projects were documented in a future-past manner where the specificity of arch tectural intervention appears as the background for fictional character narratives developed by th students centering around potential shifts in mode of future living. The proposals were present as a collective exhibition and has been interrogated in a science fair review format where studer could hone, alter and adjust their positions as critique fostered an instant feedback-loop.

DIS-COVERING THE RING-ROAD
Anna Pla Català

LOLUX HUB
Jonas Coersmeier

Architectural Association School of Architecture in London (Hons Finalist), Master of Science in Advanced Architectural Design from Columbia GSAPP via Fulbright, Founder of APC_Studio in Barcelona, Spain

Founded Büro NY (2014). MS.Arch from Columbia University (2000). Dipl.-Ing. from TU-Darmstadt (1998), M.I.T. (1996). Awarded: Young Artist Award (Association of German Architects NRW), Kinne Fellow Prize, Lowenfish Prize for Design, Honor Award for Excellence in Design (Columbia University), World Trade Center Memorial Design Award, DAAD Scholar. Coordinates Architecture and Urban Design Program (MSAUD) at Pratt Institute

Urban ring-roads exist in many cities and as much as they were a popular mechanism for reducing vehicular traffic in their central areas, their capacity has proven to be ephemeral and short lived. Today, ring-roads are questioned altogether because of their environmental impact as well as for the discontinuities they generate in the urban continuum. The space immediately adjacent to the ring-road has consolidated and caused transformations both desired and undesired, raising the need for the reformulation of its adjacent areas. To reflect upon the ring road implies the re-definition of the use of the (private) vehicle and on the pollution limits, but also the necessity of understanding the existing infrastructure as a space that holds the potential of becoming inhabitable space. The research goal is to propose new scenarios, proposals and imaginaries around the ring-road in order to raise new questions and challenges that will be the center of debate in the next years.

The architectural design studio LoLux Hub invents typologies for ultra-luxury and low-income housing, and it proposes a new type of mixed-use transport hub in Brooklyn, New York.

The studio encourages the discussion of socio-economic and political issues of urban housing, and how they relate to architectural responsibilities and desires. It promotes the idea that design holds the potential for improving human coexistence, and that it does so through the production of core architectural qualities. Architecture itself provides cultural content, creates spatio-material and aesthetic value and thus improves the urban condition.

We take a proactive approach to adaptive reuse, allowing for radical urban and architectural interventions. We consider this a form of "real" preservation, which is forward looking, as it creates a new life cycle for the existing building structure.

TENTCITY
Scott Erdy

CREATIVE INCLUSIONARY HOUSING: RED HOOK GRAIN TERMINAL
Ben Krone

Founding partner of Erdy McHenry Architecture, PA (1998), M.Arch from Syraccuse University (1990), BSC Architecture from The Ohio State University (1987), AIA Philadelphia Gold Medal (2001), AIA Philadelphia Silver Medal (2004)

Graduated highest honors Columbia University 2004, Recipient of the Mckim prize Columbia University 2004, Practiced with SHoP Architects 2001- 2007, Owner/ Founder of Gradient Architecture 2006- current

As a response to the unsheltered epidemic, the homeless in Philadelphia and other locations across the country have resorted to living in "Tent Cities." These self-organizing settlements, sometimes described as "urban camping," have helped the homeless form supportive communities where they are able to sleep in modest shelters, maintain minimal levels of security and are able to share limited resources. These encampments are nearly always established in distressed urban areas and exist in and around derelict or abandoned buildings.

The studio worked with Project HOME, a local Philadelphia Housing initiative that provides housing opportunities for those in need. Representatives of Project HOME acted as our client for the semester, providing valuable feedback on the proposals, exposing students to real-world requirements that challenged their skills as a designer and architect dedicated to serving a higher social good.

The 50,000-square-foot Transitional Housing building program was designed in accordance with the needs of Project HOME, including a range of unit types, amenities, training and social support spaces geared to assist residents in their long-term transition away from homelessness. The project will address the 1900 Block of Huntington Avenue in Philadelphia. One third of the project program will interact directly with the existing structure with the remaining 2/3 of the program area being new construction. This will encourage the production of hybrid forms, programs and architectural conditions that interrogate relationships between new and existing urban artifacts. The project also creates a safe haven for temporary encampments by providing a safe, organized and defensible precinct for campers that will help draw them closer to desperately needed transformational assistance.

Housing for lower income groups is an enormous issue nationwide. Upscale and profitable development often undermines efforts to sanction land use to house families at or below the poverty line. For decades cities have been trying to figure out ways to deal with the issue.

One such example is "Inclusionary housing where developers are incentivized to provide a stipulated amount of lower income units in exchange for tax credits and relaxed zoning regulations that may significantly increase profits on a given plot of land. However, this has not been without controversy. One big issue with these mixed income developments has been how "integration" is achieved.

Further complicating these issues are groups that exist right along the poverty line who may not be employed but not able to afford market-rate rents that these gentrifying neighborhoods demand. The shifting economics of big cities are rapidly pushing these groups of people further away from their cultural centers, stripping cities of their character and homogenizing neighborhoods toward the privileged. This semester we will focus our attention on these board line income groups and focus on a particular neighborhood currently under pressures of these forces.

ADAPTIVE MISUSE
Brian Phillips

Founded Interface Studio
Architects (ISA), Philadelphia
(2004), Master of Architecture
Weitzman School (1996), BSED
University of Oklahoma (1994),
AIA Philadelphia Gold Medal
(2018), AIA National Housing
Award (2017), Architectural
League of NY – Emerging Voices
(2015), Pew Fellowship in the
Arts (2011)

s old, former industrial cities re-emerge as creative
conomy and lifestyle hubs, formerly industrial
uildings and fabric are being re-imagined as new
cations for living, working and entertainment.
hiladelphia, as a global powerhouse of early 20th-
entury industry, has an extraordinary volume
f former industrial structures. These structures,
nce dedicated to the manufacture of hats, tex-
es, and locomotives are now providing fascinat-
g adaptive opportunities. Adaptation is potent
r several reasons—it stores cultural identity and
haracter while also creating a canvas for old
nd new to negotiate fresh relationships—through
rogram, form and material.

   This studio will offer a critique of adaptive re-use
candard procedures. The studio values existing
tructures for how they can be relevant to the present
nd future and create novel hybrids. Projects look
o connect with deep aspects of existing conditions
nd elevate them as defining characteristics.

SHIFTING HYBRIDS: ADAPTIVE REUSE ON THE LOWER EAST SIDE OF NYC

Hina Jamelle

Caleb Ehly

CRITIC: HINA JAMELLE

This housing intervention captures the dialogue between an existing structure and the forward pushing city. Within a serious of furls and protrusions, out blooms a new housing typology, one that adorns and cradles the existing theater while emerging as its own whole. On one side generating a new speculative future, while on the other side celebrating the heritage of network and the lower eastside. The rejuvenation and revitalization of the existing program and architecture space of the theater allows for a new dialogue for Lower East Side.

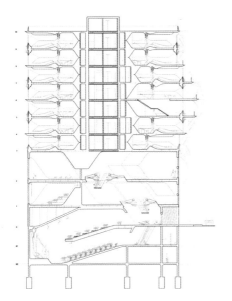

SHIFTING HYBRIDS:
ADAPTIVE REUSE ON THE
LOWER EAST SIDE OF NYC
Hina Jamelle

Jiachang Ye

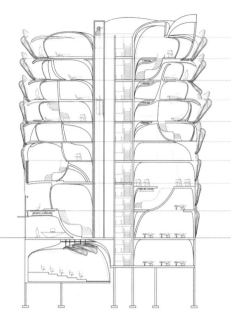

The traditional movie theater business is challenged by digital technology & people's consuming entertainment on phones & home theaters. I propose reinventing the Sun Shine Theaters to a live/work tech incubator which meets the demands of office space.

The history of the building is caped via the theater façade which is revealed through varied layers & transparence. The new adaptive building envelope will provide a vibrating, lighting & dynamic space to echo the LES neighborhood culture.

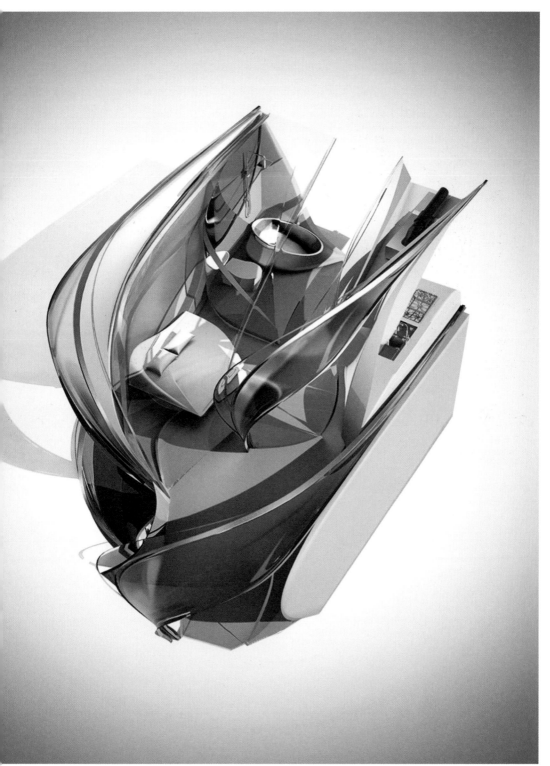

MEGA-BLOCK REDUX III
Kutan Ayata

Ryan Henriksen, Xiaotong Jiang, Ira Kapaj, Rentian Liu, Jingwen Luo, Catherine Shih, Kimberly Shoemaker, Jennifer Son, Alexa Sternberger, Sierra Summers, Tynx Taneja, Yi Wei

To treat tabula-rasa with tabula-rasa seems like a pointless exercise and a massive material waste. The studio, over the course of three years, worked collectively to speculate on Stuyvesant Town, an 18-block territory in New York City, and imagined alternative future scenarios for the next 20 years. We fully embraced the permanence of the physical context, the good, the bad, the ugly, and accepted all that it has as a 3-dimensional site to operate on. What is there remained there to initiate the next stage of urban development. We added, subtracted, intersected, fused, gutted, grew, bridged the existing typology to produce new masses, new characters. Each student generated a proposal in a specific courtyard or the building of the complex with their self-generated mix programmed housing agenda to create a heterogeneous urbanity. The collective effort of the studio aspired to transform the self-similar spatial and homogeneous urban character towards distinct moments of difference within the complex. The projects were documented in a future-past manner where the specificity of architectural intervention appears as the background for fictional character narratives developed by the students centering around potential shifts in mode of future living. The proposals were presented as a collective exhibition and has been interrogated in a science fair review format where students could hone, alter and adjust their positions as critique fostered an instant feedback-loop.

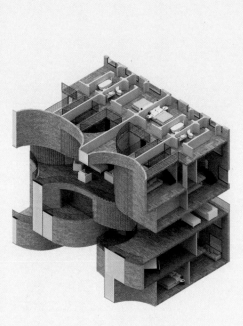

Xinyu Wang

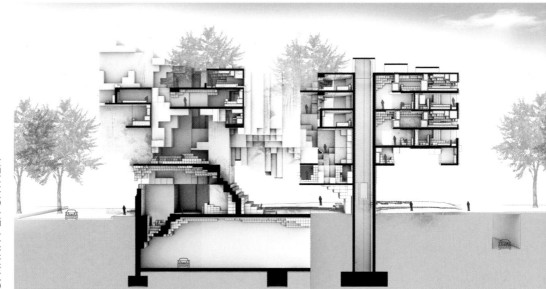

This is a project sitting somewhere between being academic and practical. Focusing on the intersection of computation and design, the project starts with its form finding process using a series of analytical and generative techniques. Attempting to incorporate the autonomous feature in the design of not only exterior form, but also the interior space, the project investigates how autonomous nature has offered new insights into aesthetics, representation, and fabrication.

DIS-COVERING THE
RING-ROAD

nna Pla Català

Suwan Park

CRITIC: ANNA PLA CATALÀ

This project aims to create a new systematic approach to engage urban public space and housing. With the use of striation, the ground system and the façade continue to develop verticality and horizontality simultaneously. The new ground system enables people to walk in from the street and leads to the view towards the sea and ring road. And it connects to the underground public swimming pool where the massive open spaces are more available. This ground condition is to be represented as the connecting point for rest of the buildings and Barcelona itself.

Julianna Cano

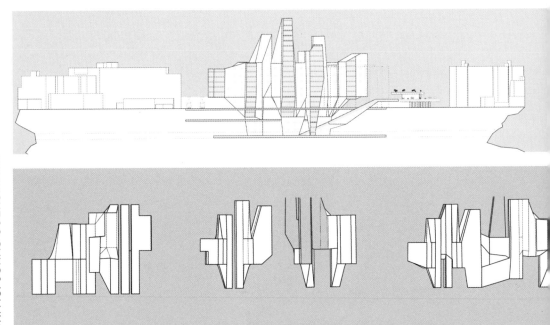

The growth of the film industry in NYC has created a sudden demand for short term housing to accommodate production crews while working on set for short, fixed amounts of time. Addressing this new demand through its dichotomous program, offering both permanent & temporary housing options for its residents. Research manifested into the creation of a central courtyard that penetrates the entire tower, creating a framework for these two conditions to merge. A microclimate is created for engagement and collaboration among the various housing typologies and post-production spaces.

LOLUX HUB
Jonas Coersmeier

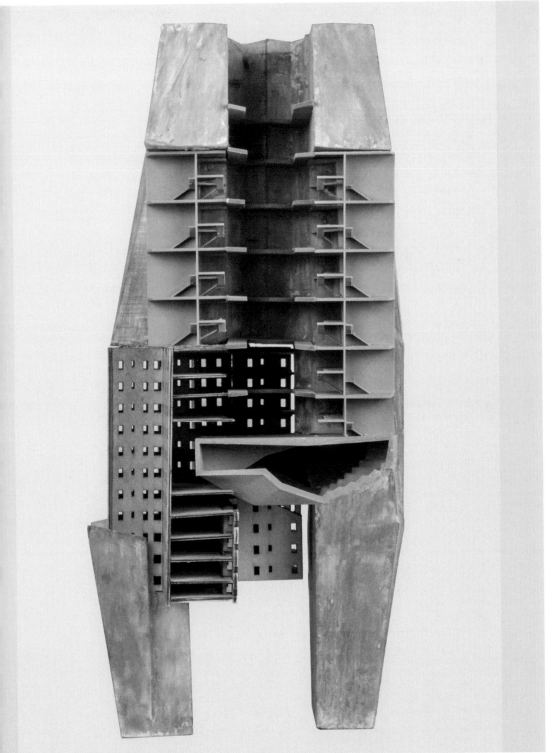

David Forero

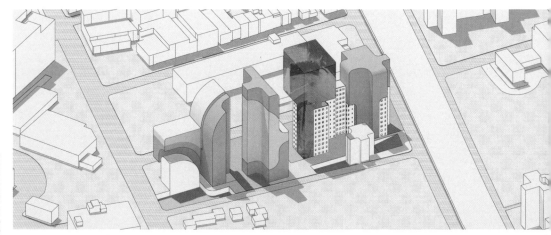

Throughout the design process the intention was to continually and strategically mix varied elements such as different materials of different densities and saturations in a casting operation to the programmatic arrangement of spaces into an existing building.

Speculation on the potential of a formal urban response derived from local adaptive reuse strategies. Through the various scales in which the project operates Admix offers an alternative approach for architectural objects to intervene in urban landscapes and critically address existing conditions.

LOLUX HUB
Jonas Coersmeier

TENTCITY
Scott Erdy

Jason Quan Hao Huynh

The project implements community centered design that provides clean water, shelter, and opportunity for the underserved. The courtyard space connects the new housing complexes above to the old existing buildings below. The void created between the old and the new is an opportunity to elevate the tent city to higher platform, which provides views, clean air, and protection.

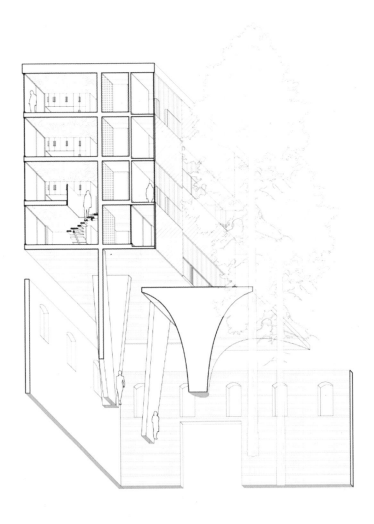

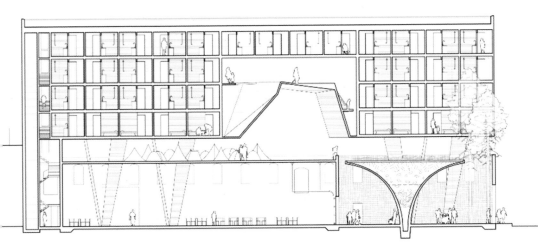

TENTCITY
Scott Erdy

CRITIC: SCOTT ERDY

Xuefeng Li

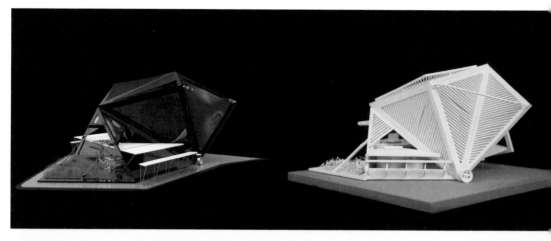

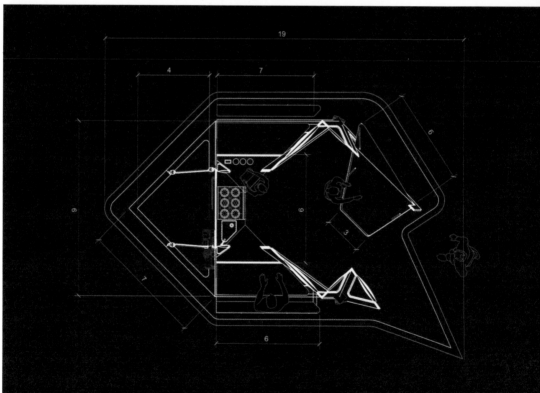

The proposed transitional housing not only provides temporary housing for the homeless population but also embarks on a memorable journey. The design proposal is an intricate network of living and social spaces integrated together, encouraging meaningful social interaction. A series of recovery programs are connected by a linear corridor and an accessible roof help to create an ascending journey. The Homeless gain new skills and physical exercise. Rocky's famous climb, a metaphor for an underdog rising to a challenge, shows it is possible for the homeless to get back on their feet.

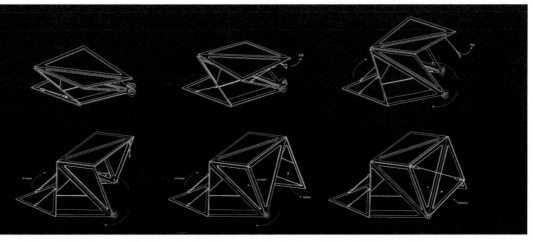

CREATIVE INCLUSIONARY HOUSING: RED HOOK GRAIN TERMINAL
Ben Krone

Chengyang Wang

By channeling silos at different levels, the confinement is broken, and the fluidity of space is created. Such manipulation is aimed to enhance communication and cooperation between young artists who have a large population base in Brooklyn. Art channeling means the dissemination of art. With the help of contemporary tools, such as social media, digital modeling software, and advanced industrial techniques, we can quickly achieve the efficiency of channeling. In my project, the redundant box of the grain terminal is utilized to provide incubators for young artists to start up their own studios.

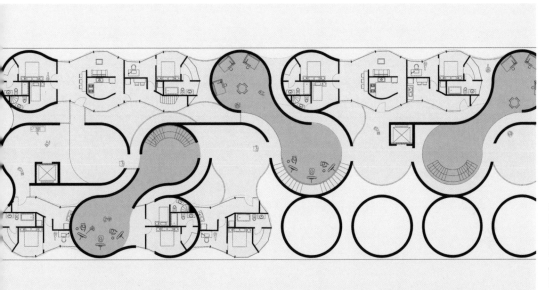

Pengkun Wang

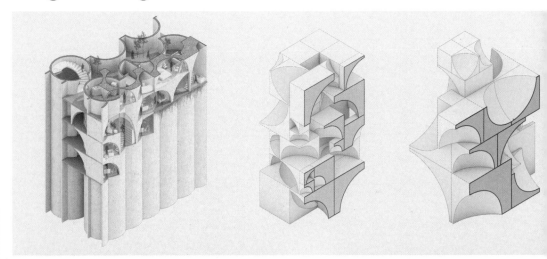

A large-area public space is formed by connection, and a small-area residential units is formed by separation. It can create open public spaces which connect people; form semi-open spaces, or completely enclosed private spaces which make area apart.

Different housing unit categories such as studio and loft can be formed by different arch aggregations. Housing units formed by small arches surround public area formed by large arches. The arrangement of these housing apartments supports the master and apprenticeship relationship.

Hongyu Li

CRITIC: BRIAN PHILLIPS

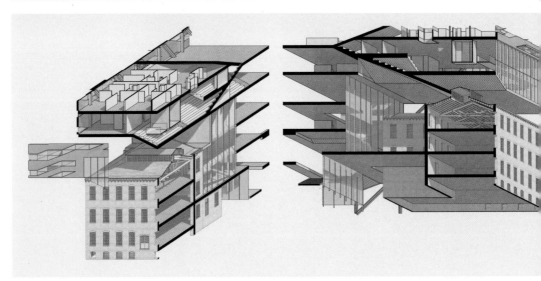

WELIVE is a contemporary working-living hub located in East Kensington, Philadelphia. The project provides a new way of working and living style that adapts to nowadays fast living pace and employment situations. It contains various housing units, office space, a courtyard and a spatial event place. Sitting between a wood-frame building and a concrete structure building, it spatially connects to the concrete building and has independent structure system to create a giant cantilever hanging above the wood-frame building, appreciating and respecting the existing architecture as well as local history.

DAPTIVE MISUSE
ian Phillips

Siyi Wang

CRITIC: BRIAN PHILLIPS

Emphasizing the relationship between old and new, as well as creating a distinctive vertical living condition to keep pace with demand and changing lifestyles, this project applies different strategies for two existing buildings. Adding new construction on the top of the concrete building, treating it as the foundation, and the other, inserting new structures into the wood structure to reinforce the existing. The grid generated by the existing buildings plays a guiding role on the arrangement of units. A new hotel and commercial program activate the block and enhance the connection with its surroundings.

DAPTIVE MISUSE

ian Phillips

57 PAVILIONS BOOK LAUNCH
AND PANEL DISCUSSION
Edited by Andrew Saunders

57 Pavilions is a 21st-century manual documenting architectural design research at Stuart Weitzman School of Design examining new potentials for part to whole assemblies where experiments in material expression, morphology, performance and culture fuse with advanced digital design processes and fabrication to produce fullscale architectural consequences. Through the presentation of 54 half-scale pavilion projects and three full-scale pavilions a novel approach is laid out for generating higher ordered physical assemblies. The formations produce a new role of parts, material processes, and aggregations yielding a more autonomous character as discrete objects in a larger assembly. As the pavilion research moves into the world in full-scale installations, these new part-to-whole relationships provoke unexpected engagement with occupants, the environment, and the larger cultural context.

57 Pavilions was released in Fall 2018 by Applied Research + Design Publishing, a sister imprint of ORO Editions.

Moderator
    Sophie Hochhäusl
    Assistant Professor for Architectural History and Theory, Weitzman School

    Introduction by Gordon Goff
    Applied Research + Design, ORO Editions, Goff Books

Panelists
    Winka Dubbeldam – Introduction and Contributor
    Miller Professor and Chair of Architecture, Weitzman School

    Andrew Saunders - Editor
    Associate Professor of Architecture, Weitzman School

    Gordon Goff
    Applied Research + Design, ORO Editions, Goff Books

    Mohamad Al Khayer - Contributor
    Lecturer, Weitzman School

    Ezio Blasetti - Contributor
    Lecturer, Weitzman School

    Danielle Willems - Contributor
    Lecturer, Weitzman School

    Michael Loverich - Contributor
    Co-Founder, The Bittertang Farm

    Eduardo Rega
    Lecturer, Weitzman School

    Abigail Coover-Hume
    Partner, Hume Coover Studio
    Co-Creator and Editor, suckerPUNCH

    Miroslava Brooks
    Founding Partner, FORMA

PENN WOMEN IN ARCHITECTURE

Formed by a group of determined female graduate architecture students in 2016, Penn Women in Architecure (PWIA) has quickly grown into a professional development powerhouse for the School and the University.

Its goal? To create a community that increases the visibility and voices of women in architecture, brings awareness to the gender disparity in the profession, and empowers female architects to grow, succeed, and become leaders in the industry.

Today, PWIA boats a mentorship program that pairs 56 students with 56 mentors in the profession—across Philadelphia, New York, and even touching the West Coast.

"I think the sooner students start getting a mentor and understanding how they can fit in and transition from academic to professional work, the sooner we're going to see our profession change in terms of how we treat equality," says Caitlin Dashiell (MArch'19), PWIA's current communications chair.

PWIA also provides various opportunities for Weitzman students to visit architecture firms, helping to boost important connections.

The group hosts events, too—both big and small. One, held on campus on April 10, featured a conversation with Madame Architect's Julia Gamolina and Winka Dubbeldam, Miller Professor and chair of architecture. During its first two years, PWIA held daylong symposiums titled "[Re]form: The Framework, Fallout & Future of Women in Design" and "[Re]action: Empowering the Future Leaders in Design."

Trubiano, a leader in architecture for many years, and a "champion" for PWIA, as the students often say, notes how impressed she has been that those who make up the group intuitively understand the gender disparities within the field, and want to make a difference.

Trubiano adds how the Graduate Architecture program at Penn is home to more than 50 percent women students. Yet, this has not yet resulted in significant shifts in architectural curricula, particularly in its ability to recognize that the education and practice of architecture is not gender neutral, Trubiano says.

Following the [Re]form and [Re]action symposia, Trubiano, along with Ramona Adlakha (MArch'18) and Ramune Bartuskaite (MArch'18), began editing a book together titled *Women [Re]build: Stories, Polemics, Futures*. It will be published by ORO Edition's AR+D Series, and available for purchase at bookstores in the fall. It features articles, interviews, and projects of leading women thinkers, activists, designers, and builders who've asked: "Where are the women in architecture?"

"There's a lack of women role models in architecture, but not because they are not there," says Adlakha. "It's because we don't hear enough about them. So, with this book, we wanted to highlight women out there doing amazing things within the profession."

Another project to come, also grown out of PWIA, focuses on 50 years of women in architecture at the School, says Trubiano. A research position next school year is being generously funded by Penn alumna Mary Keefe (W'81), of Philadelphia architecture firm MGA Partners.

- Lauren Hertzler

CORE
by Kutan Ayata, Coordinator

The Core 602 Integrative Studios simulate the collaborative environment, work-flow and output of architectural practice. Students, working as pairs and with support of various professional consultants, design and develop an architectural project towards a high degree of resolution. Our collective ambition is to maintain a high level of design rigor and utilize interdisciplinary collaboration with consultants towards experimental provocations where each discipline seeks to expand the bounds of its knowledge.

Each studio instructor defines their own brief, program and site for a building in the range of 40,000 sqft. Each studio instructor also brings in their own consultants to explore and support the polemics outlined by the studio brief. Students learn to coordinate varying pressures coming from structural, environmental and enclosure demands. What is at stake is to keep the architectural design intent intact while integrating multiple degrees of input coming from consultants. Special attention is given to the full integration of all disciplines concerned with the realization of a building, as to avoid traditional modes of consultancy which operates solely through the notions of problem solving. The students are encouraged to challenge their consultants to produce non-conventional propositions which operate under the conceptual umbrella of their projects.

Students document and represent their projects within the framework of shared base deliverables which foreground detailed line drawings. Drawings in multiple scales and resolution address questions of organization, structure, assembly, mechanical systems, materiality and aesthetics within the context of the projects' conceptual inquiries. Each section additionally work through divergent representational mediums to support the resolution and plausibility of the projects.

The semester has two coordinated studio-wide week-long exercises which focus on structure and enclosure. The Structures Week takes place few weeks before the midterm and culminates in the output of a preliminary structural strategy and its analysis. In-house faculty advise and assist the students in addition to each section's consultants. The Enclosure Week takes place few weeks after the midterm, fostering discussions in the compatibility of design intent and technical solution, again through a format of studio-wide review.

Through the semester we welcome several outside guests as part of "Master Lecture" series, who are established practitioners, exploring new frontiers in their disciplines. This past Spring, we were joined by Jesse Reiser, Principal of RUR; Sameer Kumar, Director of Enclosure at SHOP; Thorsten Helbig, Principal of Knippers Helbig Adnvanced Engineering and Drura Parrish, EVP of Xometry. During this edition of the series, each guest focused their efforts on one recent project and discussed them through all stages of design, construction and completion.

WILD THINGS
Kutan Ayata

NEWBURGH ENCLOSURES
HYPER LOCAL FOOD &
LEISURE HUB
K Brandt Knapp

Co-Founded Young & Ayata (2008) Awarded Architectural League Prize (2014), M.Arch from Princeton University (2004), BFA in Architecture from Massachusetts College of Art in Boston (1999)

Co-founder of BRANDT:HAFERI Winner of the inaugural FOLLY competition (2012), Teaches at PennDesign, Columbia's GSAPP NJIT, Pratt & Barnard, M. Arch from Yale School of Architectur (2010), B.S.D & B.A. from Arizor State University (2006)

Architecture's battle with nature is old and historically rich. The discipline of architecture has always been preoccupied with questions of representing, recreating, redefining, and embodying "nature" through various strains of its histories, i.e. from Baroque, Rococo to Art Nouveau, from Modernism, to Biomimicry, and even recent tendencies of green, sustainable approaches continue these ambitions by foregrounding responsible relations with our environment. The two most common pitfalls of all such aesthetics can be summed up as follows: either the design aims for a simulacrum of an idealized notion of "nature," resulting in literal visual interpretations of "what is commonly assumed to be natural" or aims for juxtaposition through absolute abstractions to posture against "the nature." Both these positions reflect the presumption of the commonly embraced nature/culture divide. What if we take the position that authentic "objects of nature" can be constructed and these constructions can cultivate their unique qualities, experiences, and cultures?

Our studio explored a building to house a public institution which manages, monitors, explores, studies, educates and exhibits the (counter-factual) realities of an untamed ecology of the Viaduct Rail Park in Callowhill neighborhood of Philadelphia. Formerly known as the Reading Viaduct, this piece of infrastructure was a railway which ran through various Philadelphia neighborhoods, sometimes as a tunnel, sometimes as an elevated platform. Its domestication is partly complete, its fate is sealed in usual mediocracy. We speculated on alternative potentials of its nature-artifice tensions. How does such an institution represent itself through its architecture? What is the architectural object of the urban wild life?

Speculative in nature and intending to re-imagir ecosystems and infrastructure - how we occupy and perform within them, this studio looks to th rural, urban, suburban landscapes of New York. At a time when our country has become more divisiv across these 'lines', the studio puts forth architectural propositions that grow the region and suggest Newburgh to be a hub or gateway to New York and the Hudson Valley. The site for the studi projects is located at the Short Line Transportatior Center. The imaginary of new social / spatial cor figurations around transportation and agriculture is grounded in the realities of site contexts and cur rent tech advancements. The 'food hub' brings together farmers, visitors, community members and proposes to be an education resource for the region with cooking classes and freshly growr products. It is thought to be part of the Food Justice movement that is taking place and regior ally located to connect various non-profits, such as Newburgh Urban Farm and Food Initiative. Enclo sure can be thought of in terms of a gradient - just as architecture can blur the line of 'inside' va 'outside,' the conditioned environments are studied as a network of micro-climates. The open-ai frame, the greenhouse, the regulated office or the refrigerated walk-in, investigations of the studi are looked to, to understand how it's boundaries or wall section work with collaboration and help fro the studios structural and enclosures consultants.

THE RAW THE COOKED AND THE SYNTHETIC
Nate Hume

Master of Architecture, Yale University, Partner, Hume Coover Studio, Curated Adjacencies, a group show at Yale Architecture Gallery Fall 2018, Opened Glimmering Wildness, a solo exhibition at Kent CAED Fall 2018

THE FUTURE IS TRANSPORTATION
Ben Krone

Graduated highest honors Columbia University 2004, Recipient of the Mckim prize Columbia University 2004, Practiced with SHoP Architects 2001- 2007, Owner/ Founder of Gradient Architecture 2006- current

he binary set up by Claude Levi Strauss in his
eminal work The Raw and The Cooked would
ed to be greatly expanded and splintered to under-
and the crossing of the natural and artificial
today's world. Things need to be considered not
ly in terms of material composition and origin
it also their cultural perception. Artisinal fire-
ood, mycelium bricks, ham foam, smart mud,
o grown meat; these all flicker between the natural
nd artificial illustrating a shifting sense of the
w. Many foods and materials posed as eco-friendly
nd organic are produced in labs and through
ry unnatural processes. The natural is a cultural
onstruct that is now more than ever designed
ther than found. The perception of nature and
e natural are filtered through these unnatural
rocesses arriving at foods, materials, and products
th a sense of the extra-natural. The building
dustry is ripe with new materials capitalizing on
operties from nature and new manufacturing
rocesses such as cross laminated timber and bio-
icks. Rather than searching for a natural that
es not exist, this studio will capitalize on the space
forded by these new synthetic possibilities and
e conception of new natures. The studio will launch
om Kevin Roche's Ford Foundation with its touch
 wildness contained within the building creating
 artificial garden growing through its atrium
d creating a public forest in the city block. The
terest is not in nature as decoration a la the ubiq-
tous lobby plant-wall but a building which is wild,
ing and fostering new ecologies. This will be done
rough rethinking the application of materials,
ructure, and systems to subvert traditional
naries and develop new synthesized organizations.

This studio is required to obtain a high-level understanding of this shifting transportation landscape.
The groups are asked to consider one or several
current or future transportation systems through
both historical analysis as well as researching current
trends and considerations for the future. This
research formed the foundation of each team's conceptual approach toward programming, and ultimately will be the basis for redefining the transportation
hub as a new building typology.

Although the ultimate goal of the studio is to
innovate far beyond the traditional understanding of the train station or airport, it is important
to understand their basic functions as collection
points, as well as a means of transferring between
modes of transport. Through this lens, the typology of the 'station' is a significant physical indicator
of society's reflexes. Two key recent proposals will
serve as precedents: Masdar city PRT hub, Abu Dhabi,
envisioning a carbon-zero city centered around a
new infrastructure of electric autonomous vehicles,
and Norman Foster's Modular Drone Port for
Africa's emerging economies, a completely new building typology devoted to flying autonomous vehicles.

The studio investigates both space and geometry
through careful research and experimentation into
various manual techniques of weaving, stitching,
stacking, molding and a host of other complex
structural assemblies. These will be investigated
initially at the scale of the body, involving notions
of craft and careful attention to how repetition
and technique yield complex geometric systems.
These results are embedded with the DNA for both
spatial and geometric innovation that may be
applied at various scales and utilized to test a host
of programmatic functions. The studio's research
into the physics of motion will play a crucial role
in translating small-scale geometric studies into
programmatic and spatial manifestations.

STUFF STUDIO
Daniel Markiewicz

Partner of FORMA Architects
PLLC, Co-Editor of the archi-
tecture journal: PROJECT,
M.Arch from the Yale School
of Architecture, B.S.E. in Civil
Engineering/Architecture from
Princeton University

INTRINSIC MATTER:
SPACE, STRUCTURE &
ORNAMENT
Robert Stuart-Smith

Assistant Professor of
Architecture, Stuart Weitzman
School of Design, Principal
Research Associate, University
College of London: Computer
Science, Director of The
Autonomous Manufacturing
Lab (Penn & UCL), Director of
Robert Stuart-Smith Design &
Kokkugia, M.Arch & Urbanism,
Architectural Association Scho-
of Architecture, London

As technology advances, the criteria for a building's performance increases and architects are the ones charged with the problem of what to do with this escalating amount of "stuff." Modernism and later the techno-aesthetic proposed a reductivist and abstract approach to form making as a means to reifying, at least superficially, industrial ideas of efficiency, efficacy, and performativity. While architecture has since continued to oscillate between extremes of functionalism and formalism, the ambition posited here is to find a contemporary center: Can we cultivate a formal and tectonic language that connects to the rich disciplinary history and aesthetics that can also be driven by contemporary performative metrics? Formal interests can both recall abstractions of histories, but can also evince new strategies for controlling and filtering light, mitigating the movement of water, or proposing novel techniques for ventilation.

This studio will investigate these questions through the design of a new Art School on Roosevelt Island in New York. The technical requirements for the performing and fine arts, combined with the complex development history of Roosevelt Island, will provide ample ground for exploration. Ultimately, the disciplinary task is two-fold: to cultivate a formal and architectural language which retains not only symbolic and historical systems of value, but is also capable of addressing performative functions of today. Projects must resist nostalgic tendencies to preserve or revert to old tropes of symbolism and decorum, but rather envision formal and organizational strategies with multi-layered and multi-material façade and/or building systems. The mandate put forth is thus, that form is not the product, rather it is the medium by which architecture performs; it is the mediator for space and systems, and should engage both aesthetic and technical dimensions simultaneously.

Recent developments in material technologies and robotic fabrication have enabled the design of novel hybrid objects that integrate performance and aesthetic conditions in complex ways. This challenges the designer's approach to the scale and variability of geometry within building design, and the relationship between structure, material use and design expression. From monolithic on-site construction to the prefabrication of elements or formwork, architecture cannot be designed in the same manner as a product such as a shoe architectural order must rise to additional challenges posed by the scale and complexity of the built environment.

Intrinsic Matter explored the integration of space, structure and ornament within design proposals that investigated a variable scale and intensity of design articulation within both element-scale and building scale conditions. This design exploration was pursued adjacent to one of world's most ambitious works — the Statue of Liberty. Designed by French sculptor Frédéric Auguste Bartholdi, the statue was a gift to the US from France as a gesture of friendship, in recognition of the US's successful War of Independence. The statue is a building-scale sculpture, structurally engineered by Gustav Eiffel, it is arguably one of the largest bespoke and most formally articulated works of architecture, and a suitable neighbor to the studio's designs. This year a new visitor's center will open on Liberty Island. Designed by FX Collaborative the center will house the original liberty torch and provide a educational experience of the Statue of Liberty. The studio explores alternative solutions to the visitor center by rethinking the role and design of Liberty Island itself, the removal of its cluttered support buildings, and the establishment of a dialogue between the new center and the Statue of Liberty.

HEAVY, FAST, AND RESILIENT— ONTOLOGICAL DATA FORMATIONS
Danielle Willems

Co-Founder of Mæta Design (2008). Visiting Professor at the Pratt Institute. M.Arch from Columbia University, GSAPP (2007)

This studio perceives architectural formation as part of a larger, self-organizing, adapting, material process. We started by reconsidering the Cenotaph, being both "heavy" and ancient, these impressive vessels of void, as a generative point of departure to re-conceptualize a new type of artifice in relationship to the typology of the Data Center. While engaging in the production of ontological architectural axioms through the generative capacities of algorithms in relationship to data, one focus will be the relationship between computation and machine learning. Conceptually, the Data Center and Museum will operative as a platform to explore post-human and machinic architectural space.

The studio methodology consists of three feedback layers: the material composites, generative models, and large-scale physical models. The concept of "heavy" and "fast" will be explored with a series of material/computational/electronic composites. The generative models should be a method of prototyping testing the limits of the generative diagram in order to make specific resilient spaces. The large-scale physical model component will be used as a different method of exploring, experimenting, generating architectural forms with great detail. The studio thesis will venture into an invesgation that is extremely sensitive to existing models of self-organization in material, cognition and physical data systems, the intention could not be further than the mere replication of "matter" nor "nature." On the contrary, with the deployment of non-linear computational design methodologies, this studio seeks explore new singularities in the extended territory of contemporary architectural production. At the same time, this research allows for the transcendence of traditional disciplinary architectural boundaries since our focus in complexity itself is an emergent language shared between multiple scientific and artistic fields.

WILD THINGS
Kutan Ayata

Zoe Cennami, Mo Shen

CRITIC: KUTAN AYATA

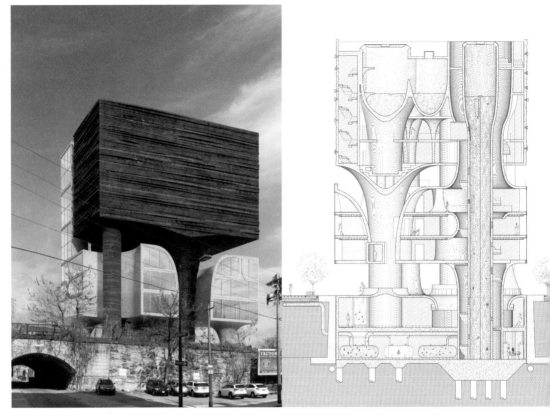

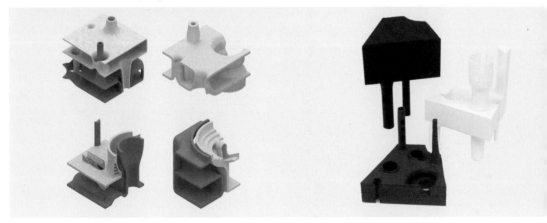

Our building blurs the boundary of what is artificial and natural by cultivating unique qualities that become the architectural object of urban wildlife. By constructing these bioluminescent pools, a freediving space, and a luminescent museum, we engage people to undermine their assumptions of the reality of the human land strata and engulf them in a new paradox of underwater experiences that are unfamiliar to our natural strata. Additionally, the glowing water from our building gets distributed throughout the rail park, lighting the space up at night.

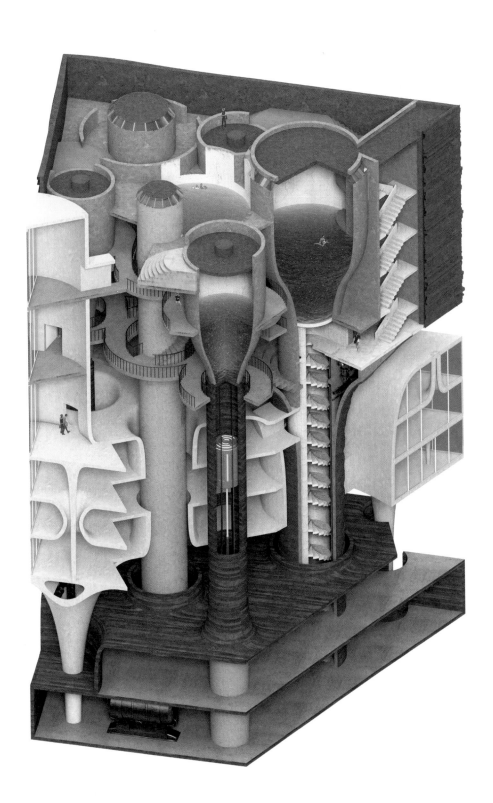

WILD THINGS
Kutan Ayata

John Dai, Chris Noh

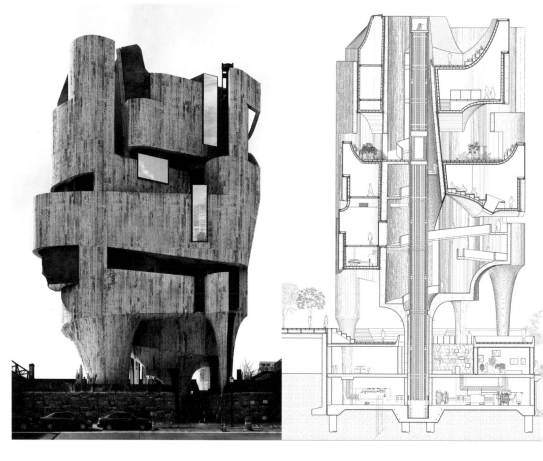

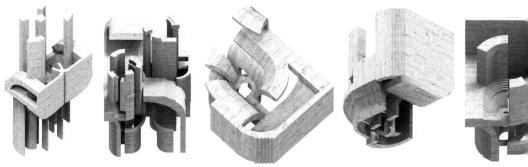

The project is an exploration of the ambiguity and juxtaposition of urban and nature conditions. The outdoor building, which functions as a vertical extension of the park creates a sequence of visualizations of artificial climates powered by a high-performance Geo-Thermal infrastructure. The building consists many enclosed "objects" that house a public institution which collects, monitors, manages and exhibits the (counter-factual) realities of an untamed ecology.

Mitch Chisholm, Angelo Spagnolo

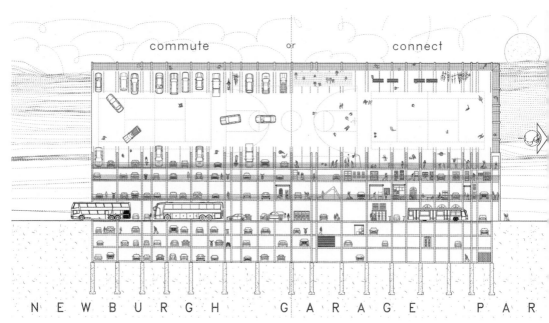

The Newburgh Commuter Park redirects vehicular and pedestrian circulation through a field of strategic encounters that invite a population pressed for time to recognize and seize opportunities for individual agency. Commuter-centered cores including a food market, daycare, library, and gym which frame new pedestrian streets and the original parking surface itself as potent sites of idea incubation and recreational pursuits.

NEWBURGH ENCLOSURES HYPER LOCAL FOOD & LEISURE HUB
K Brandt Knapp

Pengkun Wang, Xintong Zhao

The Burgeoning is an architectural proposal which speculates new modes of construction and logistics to tackle food security problems and to enrich the community identity for Newburgh. The Burgeoning, with a focus on sustainable and efficient operations, is a hub for hydroponic farms as well as delivery drones which serve fresh and locally grown produce to the community and its surroundings areas. The architecture and landscape of this hub is designed to be in a state of constant organic growth for the members of the community to gather, interact and further develop through time.

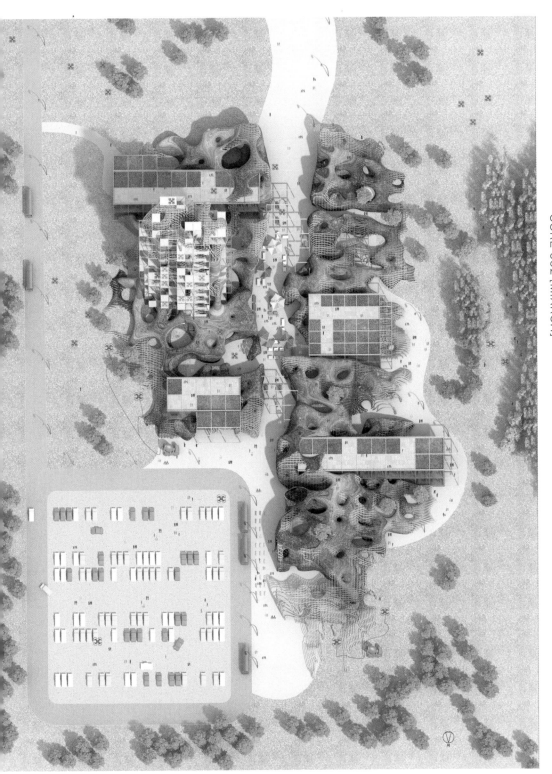

Ryan Henriksen, Kimberly Shoemaker

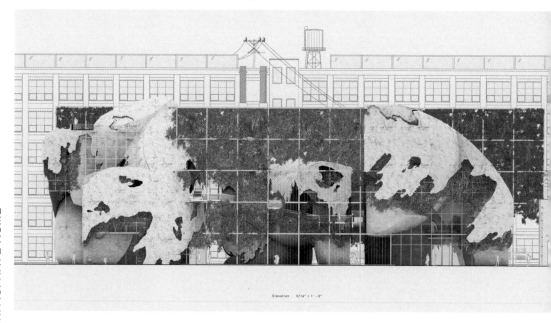

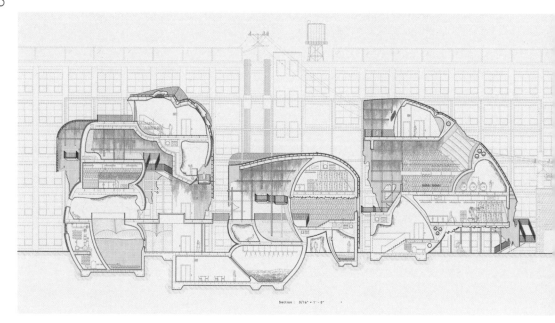

This project aims to use a layering of multiples to blur the boundaries of spatial configurations and interrogate new manipulations of threshold conditions. Multiples, which manifest themselves as interior forms, programmatic spaces, envelope overlays, material applications, and structural systems, act both formally independent and functionally dependent on one another. Overlaid, these systems of multiple autonomies blur perceptions of the whole by generating continual glimpses through and between; breaking down spatial familiarities and introducing new in-between environments.

Katarina Marjanovic, Sierra Summers

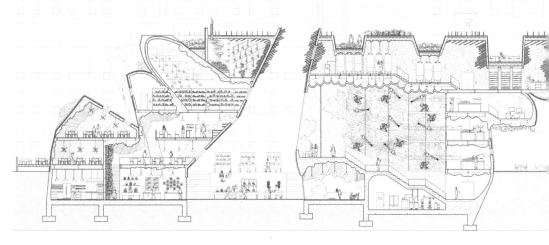

We explored materiality and its ability to deteriorate and de-familiarize form.
Layers of concrete, brick, corten, perforation, and foliage build up to create
a facade that is neither completely urban nor pastoral. For us, materiality
has evolved beyond a surface treatment. The materials become spatial
through extruded louvers and fluting. The chasm between the two buildings
creates views of connection and moments of tension. The steep cantilevers
at the front invite you in as the applique of the facade breaks down large
exterior planes.

HE RAW THE COOKED
ND THE SYNTHETIC

te Hume

CRITIC: BEN KRONE

Yaofang Hu, Jihyun Kim

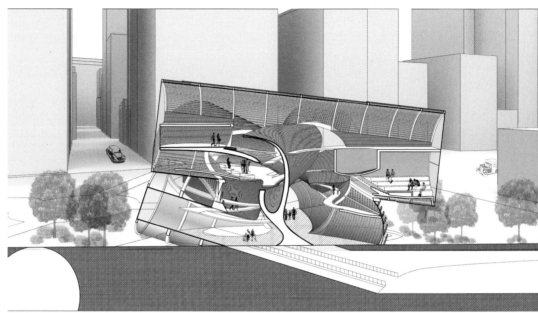

The outside tubes present the simplicity of input movement, and curved "reflectors" act as "Prisms" to conduct each input and reflect them as different outputs. We use linear and arch metal strips for the facade, which enhance the directionality of the primary tubes. The different density and orientation of strips provide shading on the ceiling and opening on walls.

THE FUTURE IS TRANSPORTATION

Ben Krone

Rui Lu, Siyi Wang

Due to the constantly changing environment and the increasing needs on efficiency in society, we believe the future of transportation should be more pedestrian focused. This project is a hub for transportation policy education and personal vehicles advocacy. The building will act like a filter and a generator that creates a shared "park" for pedestrians through program filtration, and stimulates the public moving forward toward future transport.

THE FUTURE IS TRANSPORTATION

Ben Krone

STUFF STUDIO
Daniel Markiewicz

Jingwen Luo, Qiaomu Xue

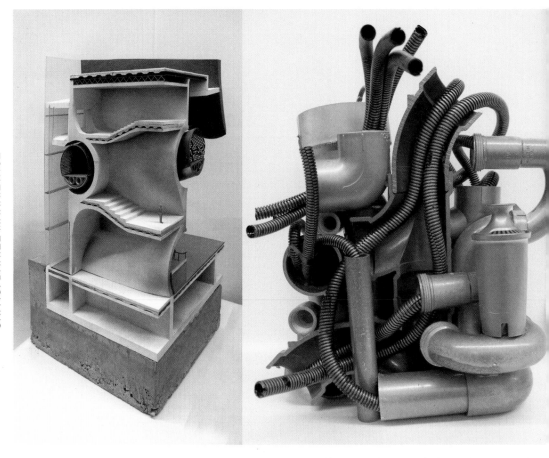

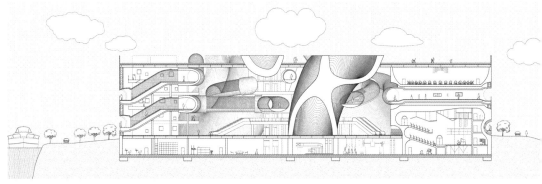

We aim to investigate intersection of form and functionality, especially industry language in the spatial dimension. The Island is adjacent to Manhattan but detached from it, which creates unique chance to design a building that is contrary to most of the buildings in Manhattan. The Arts Complex is antithesis of the buildings in Manhattan including horizontality vs. verticality, inefficiency vs. efficiency and slow vs. fast traffic. The design proposes to utilize tubes as circulatory and gallery space that provide people with a continuous and fascinating experience to connect office and performing.

STUFF STUDIO
Daniel Markiewicz

CRITIC: DANIEL MARKIEWICZ

Alexa Sternberger, Eliana Weiner

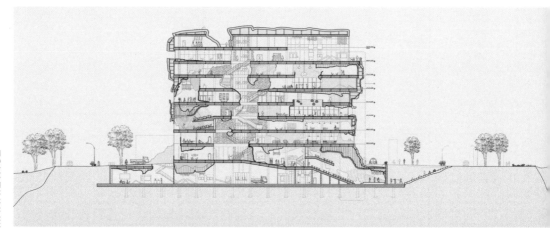

People are the carvers of stuff; they erode the rigidity of a system and break down the predetermined parameters of program. The character of the space is thus generated by the actions of the people. These carved out spaces are further articulated by the materiality and textures of the building. Using the various stones on both the exterior and interior of the building, the rocks create a continuous relationship between outside and inside, blurring the line between the edge condition of the building and that of the art space.

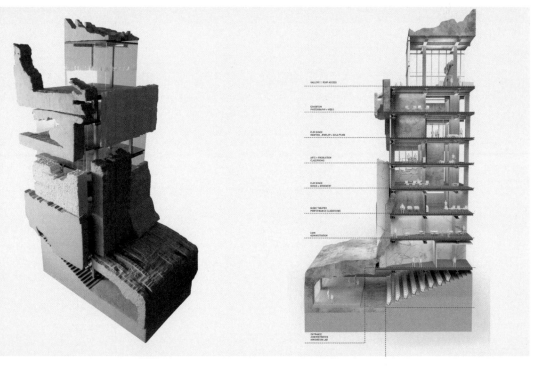

INTRINSIC MATTER: SPACE, STRUCTURE & ORNAMENT
Robert Stuart-Smith

Sien Hang Cheng, Hongyu Lin

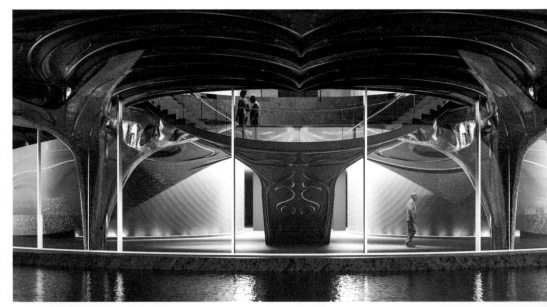

Through studying the complex formal-structural integration in the construction of the statue itself, the structure of the new visitor center aimes to incorporate space and structure through Topological Structure Optimized (TSO) form that molds a wholistic formal construction. The combination of space, structure, and ornamentation reconfigures our perception towards an integrated structure, which ultimately echoes back to the original ambition of the Statue of Liberty.

INTRINSIC MATTER: SPACE, STRUCTURE & ORNAMENT
Robert Stuart-Smith

David Forero, Ian Lai, Akarsh Sabhany

CRITIC: ROBERT STUART-SMITH

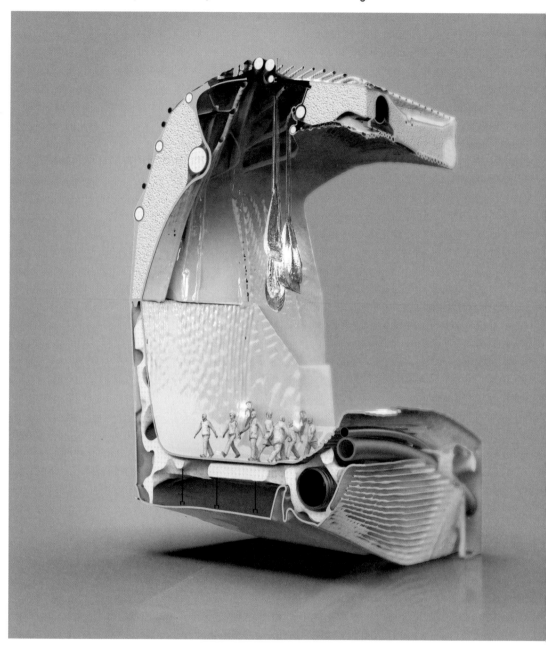

The Statue's application of novel construction methods and fabrication techniques, the project challenges contemporary construction norms, and explores alternative systems that can perform as structural and aesthetic objects. Where Bartholdi once pushed the boundaries of metal construction and geometric cladding to a worldwide pinnacle, decades have passed, and we owe it to him and his builders on take the advances of architectural design and construction to new heights for our age.

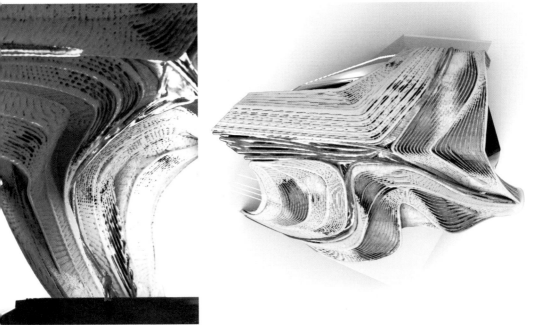

Zachary Jones, Daniel Knee

Our data center attempts to take a monolithic paradigm of inaccessible and inhuman networks of systems and machines and make this program perme-able and socially accessible. This center encourages the making of an infra-structural space into a social and cultural center which enables it to engage its surroundings. This is achieved in part by allowing the data to be directly observed and curated for the public to view. This is also achieved by allowing this data space to continue growing with the surrounding neighborhood to accommodates the new needs of new data.

HEAVY, FAST, AND RESILIENT— ONTOLOGICAL DATA FORMATIONS

Danielle Willems

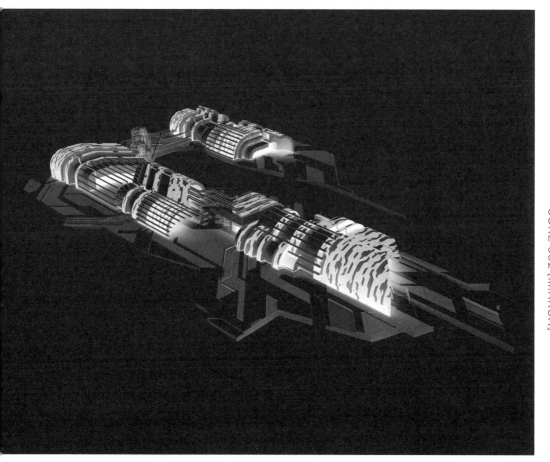

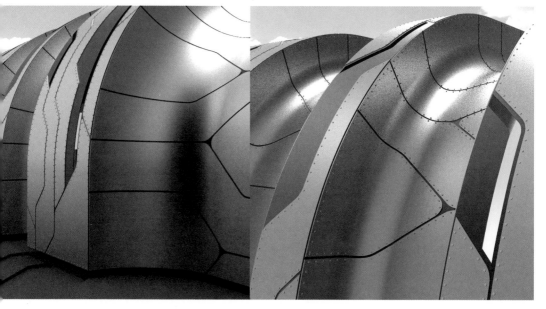

Joonsung Lee, Jennifer Minjee Son

CRITIC: DANIELLE WILLEMS

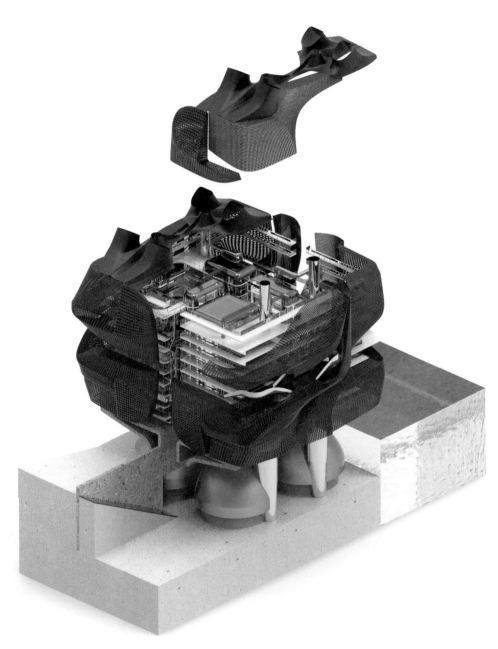

The definition of Mismatch is "a failure to correspond or match; a discrepancy" or "a faulty or unsuitable match." However, mismatch is not always used as negative meaning, but sometimes it is used positively as well. For instance, in fashion, mismatch is used when two different things matched and it creates something different which did not exist before. Our project is also following the concept of two different programs combined in a unique way to create new things.

EAVY, FAST,
ND RESILIENT—
NTOLOGICAL
ATA FORMATIONS

nielle Willems

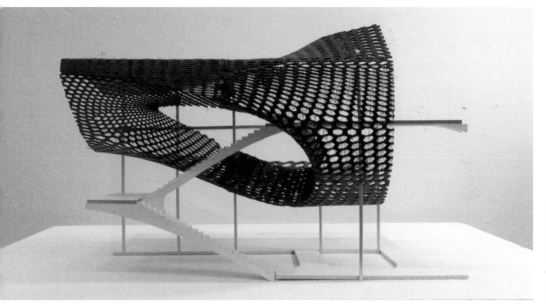

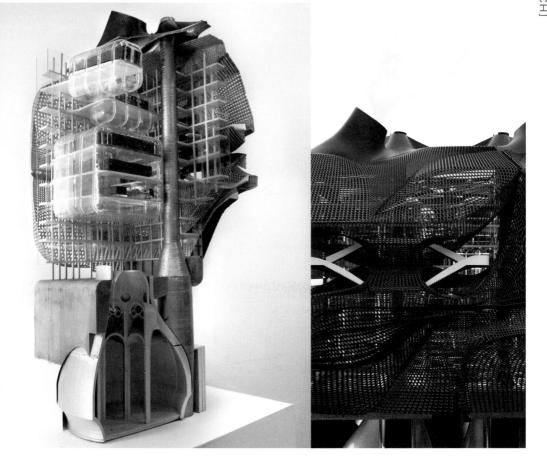

GALLERY

hengyang Wang
ritic: Ben Krone

Qiaomu Xue
Critic: Ben Krone

Amanda Gruen and Karen Toomasian
Critic: Kutan Ayata

sui-Lun Wang and Xinyu Wang
ritic: Robert Stuart-Smith

Alexa Sternberger and Eliana Weiner
Critic: Daniel Markiewicz

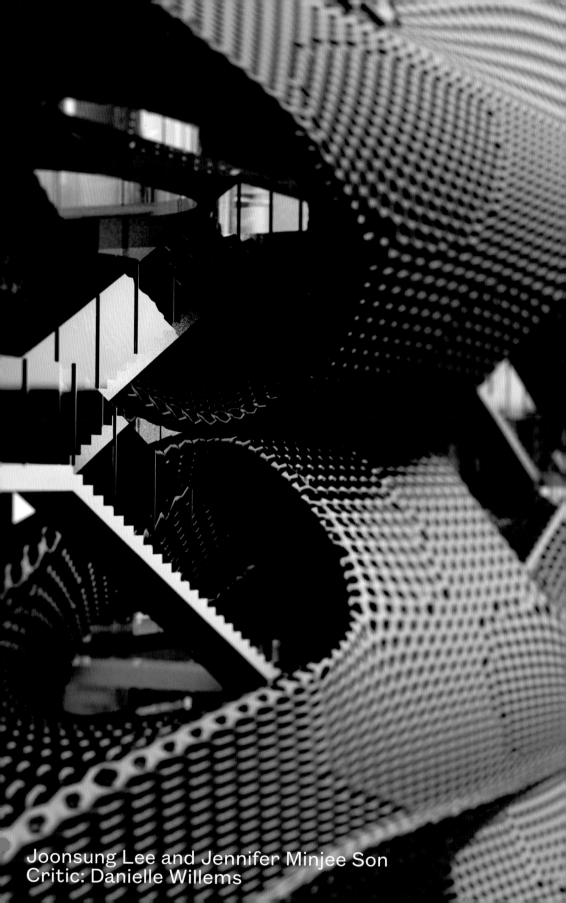

Joonsung Lee and Jennifer Minjee Son
Critic: Danielle Willems

SPRING NEWS

JANUARY 2019

WINKA DUBBELDAM SPEAKS AT ZHEJIANG UNIVERSITY IN CHINA

Miller Professor and Chair of Architecture Winka Dubbeldam traveled to Hangzhou, China to participate in the "Neo-Build Forum" at the Architectural Design and Research Institute of Zhejiang University (UAD). She also gave a lecture and discussed potential collaborations between the University and the Weitzman's School's Advanced Research & Innovation Lab (ARI).

Dubbeldam recently won the Asian Games Sports Park Competition 2018 in Hangzhou with her office Archi-Tectonics. She and her team designed a mile long park, two stadiums, a shopping mall, and visitor center. The park will open in March 2021.

DESIGNS FOR MAKING THE ARCHIVE VISIBLE

As one of the world's great archeology and anthropology research museums, and the largest university museum in the United States, the Penn Museum houses over a million objects, some dating back several millennia. But this week, through a partnership with the Weitzman School, the Museum is displaying a collection of objects made just weeks ago.

The objects are the work of first-year graduate architecture students who were asked to imagine a 42,000-square-foot addition to the museum, in the Stoner Courtyard, that would integrate collections storage, gallery, and event spaces. Their assignment, for the 501 Studio, addresses the reality that although the Museum's collection contains over a million artifacts, only about 3% of them are on display.

Each of the seven sections of the studio approached the project in different ways, focusing on different issues. Some designs explored the possibilities of making collections storage much more visible to visitors, or "making the withdrawn nature of the archive visible," as Andrew Saunders, associate professor of architecture and the studio coordinator for ARCH 501, puts it.

The design by one student, Huadong Lin, takes its form directly from objects in the Museum's collections. "The shapes of the

structures I designed trigger your imagination by alluding to the prehistoric forms that you see in the collection," says Lin.

Other designs take on reimagining the form and function of the Museum's Stoner Courtyard, which resembles a bucolic Italian villa decorated with sculptural pieces by A.S. Calder, despite being hemmed in by University buildings. "The courtyard of the museum has high walls. I wanted to break this boundary so I made the archive tall. From the top visitors can see both the city skyline and the landscape of the campus," explains Yuhao Zhang about his project. "I also designed the spaces outside of the buildings so that the courtyard itself functions as a public space for people to gather."

The ways that the role of the collection has evolved at the Museum, and its approach to acquiring material, was another theme that runs through many of the designs, according to Saunders. "The Museum is not acquiring in the ways it did when it was founded," he says. "It is no longer an open vessel to be filled. The main function of the archive is now acting as an interface between scholars and the public with this enormous collection."

The designs on view were selected by the Museum's executive team, including the Merle-Smith Director of Learning Programs Ellen M. Owens. "Many designs responded to the Museum's remit to work with the public, which is a top priority for us," noted Owens. "The thoughtful treatment of how these structures would enhance public engagement was the center of our proposal discussion."

Selected:
  Alan Fan
  Lingxin Feng
  Huadong Lin
  Sami Samawi
  Yi-Hsuan Wu
  Yuhao Zhang
  Jingyi Zhou

Finalists:
  Maria Fuentes
  Madison Green
  Matt Kohman
  Paul McCoy
  Veronica Rosado
  Megan York
  Tianhui Zhang

FEBRUARY 2019

WINKA DUBBELDAM AND FERDA KOLATAN LECTURE IN ISTANBUL

Miller Professor and Chair of Architecture Winka Dubbeldam and Associate Professor of Practice

Ferda Kolatan lectured in Istanbul on Februar[y] and 15 at events hosted by Global Architectu[re] Development (GAD).

Dubbeldam shared her latest researc[h] "New Solids," on Friday, February 15 at the Istanbul Technical University. In October 2[018] she was invited to give a related lecture at SCI-Arc.

Kolatan discussed "Real Fictions," a the[me] of his 700-level studios, on Tuesday, Februar[y] at Kadir Has University. His 2017 studio, "Re[al] Fictions Cairo," won an AIA Studio Prize and [was] featured on the cover of *Architect* magazine[.]

WEITZMAN SCHOOL FACULTY WIN ANNUAL PROGRESSIVE ARCHITECTURE (P/A) AWARDS

Three Weitzman School faculty members hav[e] been selected for 2019 Progressive Architect[ure] (P/A) Awards from the American Institute of Architects. Now in its 66th year, the awards recognize unbuilt projects demonstrating ove[rall] design excellence and innovation. Their work will be published in the February 2019 issue o[f] *ARCHITECT*, and honored at a celebration in New York in February 2019. The jury selected [?] projects from nearly 200 submissions.

Senior Lecturer Kutan Ayata received [an] Award for the DL 1310 Apartments in Mex[ico] City. A collaboration between his firm Your[s] Ayata and Michan Architecture, it was one [of] only two Award recipients.

The DL 1310 Apartments were descri[bed] by jury critic J. Frano Violich as, "provid[ing a] sense of thickness and depth that is very s[kill]ful and super effective."

The design is the product of extensive research into the technical capabilities of [?] and local traditions in concrete, recalling th[e] gemoetries of Félix Candela and Miguel Fisa[c to] solve challenges.

Additionally, Cret Chair of Professor [?] of Practice Thom Mayne's firm Morphosis received an Honorable Mention for the Orange County Museum of Art in Costa Me[sa,] California.

Lecturer Paul Preissner also received an Honorable Mention for Ring of Hope in Chicago. It was submitted by his firm Paul Preissner Architects.

WEITZMAN SCHOOL STUDENTS WIN 2019 HOK FUTURES DESIGN CHALLENGE

For the second year in a row, Master of Architecture students made a clean sweep[?]

HOK Futures Design Challenge. All three he finalist spots were awarded to teams of zman School students:

t Place:
  Team Son & Lee - Jennifer Minjee Son (MArch'20) & Joonsung Lee (MArch'20)

ond Place:
  Team Faint Fable - Patrick Danahy (MArch'20) & Caleb Ehly (MArch'20)

d Place:
  Team .MPA - Paul McCoy (MArch'21) & Madison Green (MArch'21)

 in its third year, HOK Futures invites adelphia-area architecture students to pete for internships and cash prizes. The ee finalists presented their entries to local ign and development professionals at an rds ceremony in HOK's Philadelphia. This is ahy and Ehly's second year as finalists. The 2018 finalists were also all Weitzman ool students:

t Place:
  "River Gate" by John Dai (MArch'20) and Xiangyu Chen (MArch'20)

ond Place:
  "A Fantastical Fiction of the Lighthouse's Furnace" by Patrick Danahy (MArch'20) & Caleb Ehly (MArch'20)

d Place:
  "Non-End" by Yefan Zhang (MArch'19) and Yi Zhang (MArch'19)

STUDENT MAGAZINE BABBLE RELEASES INAUGURAL ISSUE

 inaugural issue of *Babble* was published in ruary by graduate architecture students. nded in 2017, the magazine provides a look he Weitzman School's diversified approach rchitectural making, thinking, and practic- by presenting a spectrum of student ects and essays paired with a series of romptu "babbles" with critics, faculty, and ctitioners.

In this issue, students were prompted to mit a single project image with a statement ts meaning to them. The student editors spoke with faculty and visiting critics "to ablish formal conversations that would ack the diverse fields of interests that ke up our school's pedagogical approach."

The *Babble* team also recently organized xhibition, *On Models*, at the Philomathean iety's Art Gallery in College Hall.

Team: Ryan Barnette, Keven Bloomfield, chell Chisholm, Caitlin Dashiell, Caleb Ehly, dison Green, Celia Y. Hao, Nikita Jathan, Ira aj, Megan Khunakridatikarn, Ian Lai, Dani ds, Andrew Matia, Paul McCoy, Kurt Nelson, y Polk, Peik Shelton, and Megan York

---

MARCH 2019

ALI RAHIM HOSTS ARCHITECTURE PANEL IN BEIJING

Professor of Architecture Ali Rahim, Professor of Architecture and Urban Design and Former Dean Marilyn Jordan Taylor, and Professor and Chair of Landscape Architecture Richard Weller hosted a two-day event called the Penn-China Design Dialogues in Beijing, with three panels focused on urban design, architecture, and landscape architecture.

The architecture panel explored questions about how technology has transformed architecture in China, how it has given architects new capacities as designers and where they are still limited, and what promises of digital architecture remain unfulfilled, Rahim says. He gathered the most influential architects and design educators in China, and their diverse set of experiences, opinions, and scales of work created a rich discussion on the panel. Panelists included China-based architects, scholars from Tsinghua and Tongji universities, and the dean of the Chinese Academy of Fine Art.

APRIL 2019

PHD CANDIDATE EARNS DAAD RESEARCH GRANT

Liyang Ding, PhD Candidate in the History and Theory of Architecture, was awarded a Research Grant from the German Academic Exchange Service (DAAD). The funding will allow him to continue his doctoral research on German architect Hans Scharoun at the Architectural Archive of the Academy of Fine Arts in Berlin in 2019-2020. Liyang's research aims to provide a critical account of the role of Chinese architecture and urban culture played in Scharoun's work, his evolving conception of architectural space, and Asian-European exchange in general. Founded in 1925, the DAAD is a registered members association made up of German institutions of higher education and student bodies. Entirely financed from federal public funds, the Research Grants are awarded to highly qualified candidates who have already proven their academic competency and plan to gain international research experience in Germany as well as worldwide.

WINKA DUBBELDAM LECTURE AND EXHIBITION AT THE UNIVERSITY OF ILLINOIS

On Monday, April 15, Miller Professor and Chair of Architecture Winka Dubbeldam presented her new lecture "Protocities,

---

Protobuilding, Prototypes" at the University of Illinois at Urbana-Champaign. She was invited to speak by Aaron Paul Brakke, a former collaborator at her firm, Archi-Tectonics. Brakke is now an assistant professor at the University of Illinois. Some panels from Dubbeldam's exhibition "Downtown Bogotá // My Ideal City" were also be on display. The exhibition premiered at the Aedes Architecture Forum in Berlin, Germany in 2013.

MAY 2019

BRIAN PHILLIPS WINS NATIONAL AIA HOUSING AWARD

Lecturer and alumnus Brian Phillips's firm Interface Studio Architects (ISA) has won a 2019 National Housing Award from the American Institute of Architects (AIA). His project, Tiny Tower, is one of two award recipients in the "One- and Two-Family Production Homes" category, one of 16 total recipients, and the only project in Pennsylvania. Tiny Tower previously won an AIA Philadelphia Honor Award in the Built category.

ALUMNUS WINS ARCHIPRIX INTERNATIONAL HUNTER DOUGLAS AWARD

Weitzman School alumnus Gary Polk (MArch'18) was awarded a 2019 Archiprix International Hunter Douglas Award in Santiago, Chile. His design, Synthetic Cultures, was one of 7 finalists out of 407 nominees from around the world. He was the only representative from the United States. Of Polk's work, the jury said, "The narrative is a wonderful 'sci-fi' project. Not every project has to be plausible, and this one takes you out of your comfort zone." Associate Professor Simon Kim served as an advisor for Synthetic Cultures.

ARCHITECTURAL THEORY NOW?
SYMPOSIUM, APRIL 4-5, 2019

The Architecture department at the Weitzman School hosted an international conference dedicated to the question of *Architectural Theory Now?* in the twenty-first century. Is the field at an impasse, or is it passé? Not only are many print journals important to the field now gone, architectural theory courses have been eliminated in many schools' curricula in favor of technology-centered courses, research studios, history without theory, and autonomous theory. It's as if architectural theory, a field of inquiry developed and articulated over a few thousand years, filling archives and rare book rooms with beguiling works of architectural knowledge, was suddenly transformed in unrecognizable ways.

Paper presenters and conversants including Francesca Hughes, Jonathan Massey, Joan Ockman, Jane Rendell, Adam Sharr, Michael Benedikt, Michael Cadwell, Jon Yoder, Lynnette Widder, Terrance Galvin, Jonathan Hale, and Juan Heredia were invited to comment on the current state of affairs and to envision a possible return to an operative or reflective practice of theory.

Each were asked to respond, challenge, and hopefully even ignore one of three working themes. *Within/Without* which challenged architectural theory's dual origins in ideas internal to the discipline of architecture and in principles and contexts far beyond it; *Practices* which discussed contemporary methods, performances, engagements, and enactments of architectural theory as defined through the lens of writers, philosophers, and theorists; and *Re-Definitions* which expanded the very characterization of architectural theory by introducing and discussing the value of alternative subjects, visions and actions. The outcomes of the symposium will be published in a forthcoming book.

ORGANIZERS
Franca Trubiano (Weitzman School)
David Leatherbarrow (Weitzman School)
Peter Laurence (Clemson University)

NEW PROGRAM: MASTER OF SCIENCE IN DESIGN IN ARCHITECTURAL DESIGN, ROBOTS, AND AUTONOMOUS SYSTEMS (MSD-RAS) BEGINNING IN FALL 2020

Directed by Assistant Professor Robert Stuart-Smith, this new year-long MSD explores avenues for re-situating the role of architectural design and the architect within present day autonomous technologies, where architecture can critically engage with novel forms of architectural design, manufacturing, construction, occupation, demolition and re-use.

Students will develop skills in advanced forms of robotic manufacturing, artificial intelligence and vision technologies to develop methods for design that harness production as a creative opportunity.

Operating predominantly through design studios, participants will critically assess the socio-political, ethical and philosophical dimensions of a recent societal shift towards algorithmic and autonomous technological dependence, and attempt to provoke alternative forms of dialogue with industry and culture that address our individual and collective engagement with the built environment. The work of the program will be both highly speculative and physically manufactured. Students will collaboratively develop robotically manufactured architectural prototypes (part or whole) at full scale that will be presented and exhibited at the completion of the course.

Robert Stuart-Smith is also the director of the Autonomous Manufacturing Lab, which explores the integration of design and production within robotic processes of building manufacturing. The interdisciplinary AML lab aims to develop innovative methods of autonomous and semi-autonomous bespoke fabrication that leverage real-time robotics, computation, sensor and computer vision technologies within generative design processes. It is part of the Weitzman's School Advanced Research and Innovation Lab (ARI), led by Miller Professor and Chair of Architecture Winka Dubbeldam.

SIR PETER COOK WORKSHOP

Graduate Architecture had the honor of hosting Sir Peter Cook for the EwingCole Lecture and a three-day studio workshop for 500-level students.

Sir Peter Cook is the founder of Archigram and the Cook-Robotham Architecture Bureau (CRAB) Studio, and former Chair of The Bartlett School of Architecture. A Graduate of the Bournemouth College of Art and the Architectural Association in London, he has been a pivotal figure within the architectural world for 50 years.

His EwingCole lecture, titled "Dreams – Realities – Explorations," examined his creative process over the span of his career.

Peter also led a studio workshop for all 500-level students, overseen by Associate Professor Andrew Saunders and the first-year faculty. Over 80 students presented their drawings and models for vessels, which were inspired by work in the Penn Museum's collection. These vessels will then become proposals for full-scale pavilion installations.

Associate Professor Annette Fierro invited Peter to visit her seminar, Archigram and Its Legacy: London, A Techtopia, which focuses on the studio he founded.

Miller Professor and Chair of Architecture Winka Dubbeldam also arranged a visit to Louis Kahn's Esherick House and Robert Venturi's Mother's House with William Whitaker, the Curator and Collections Manager of our Architectural Archives.

AD
NC

VA
ED'

ADVANCED'

by Winka Dubbeldam, Coordinator
Miller Professor and Chair of Architecture

THE MASSIVE

This third-year elective design-research studio is focused on the massive: very large-scale architecture and its somewhat strained relationship with the urban surroundings. The idea is to move beyond traditional planning to pro-pose different scenarios and new interfaces where city and building meet. We propose it is not the masterplan that drives the development of the city any-more, but a bottom-up scenario that can instigate and cause spontaneous growth. This not only creates super large structures, but also impacts social, cultural, and economic growth--hence directly impacting the city around itself. Bruce Mau states in his *Incomplete Manifesto for Growth*:

Allow events to change you. You have to be willing to grow. Growth is different from something that happens to you. You produce it. You live it. The prereq-uisites for growth: the openness to experience events and the willingness to be changed by them. Forget about good. Good is a known quantity. Good is what we all agree on. Growth is not necessarily good. Growth is an exploration of unlit recesses that may or may not yield to our research. As long as you stick to good you'll never have real growth.

DESIGN-RESEARCH

Our diverse and renowned faculty create an amazing range of studios provoking the normative. Themes like "the large and the futuristic" are found in the studios led by Thom Mayne ("Tencent, the future Sci-Tech"), Ferda Kolatan ("Oddkin architecture / Galataport Istanbul"), and Iñaki Echeverria ("Hacking Infra-structure/ Radical Hybrids"), while other studios propose a resilient future, like Matthijs Bouw's "Highways to Resilience" and Joe Mac Donald's "Sustainable Evolutions Dubai." The role of the object as a critical and massive architecture can be found in Simon Kim's "Montreal, the Sensate and Augmented," Paul Preissner's "Dirts and Rocks and Maybe Logs and Things," Robert Stuart-Smith's "Les Halles, 2030 Post Humanist Space," and Georgina Huljich's "Autonomous and Authentic or Historical and Vernacular."

The studio's goal is not to propose a new type or typology, but to create productive responses and provocations that negate the existing urban condi-tion, or suggest a transformative relationship between the object and the context, or from the object to itself.

GLOBAL INITIATIVES

An integral part of the 701 studio is collaboration with the real world: external experts that support and collaborate with the studio, like governments, developers, and other universities. They have become an integral part of how the studios operate by inviting students to visit and perform in-depth research locally. Our past successes in international partnerships have led to several recent requests for collaboration, like a three-year design-research project with the Government of Egypt looking at the informal areas and infra-structures in Old Cairo, a collaboration with the R&D group of Cemex in Biel, Switzerland, a collaboration with an architect in Istanbul, a developer in Cartagena, Colombia, and a developer in Mexico. Student work from these collaborations have since been exhibited in the Egyptian Pavilion at the 2016 Venice Architecture Biennale, 2017 Seoul Biennale, and the 2018 Venice Architecture Biennale. These are just a few examples of our research projects and collaborations led by faculty and visiting faculty, many of whom are steadily becoming part of our team of returning guest critics.

HIGHWAYS TO RESILIENCE
Matthijs Bouw

Associate Professor Practice, Rockefeller Urban Resilience Fellow, McHarg Center Fellow Risk and Resilience, Founder o One Architecture

Superstorm Sandy showed just how vulnerable New York City is to flooding. Much of the city is built in the floodplain, often on former marshes or on reclaimed land. NYC coastal zones have been especially important as the location for the infrastructure of the modern city: logistics and manufacturing, energy facilities and waste water treatment plants, transportation terminals, and, from the mid 20th century, highways. By the late 20th century, much of the waterfront had been disconnected from the urban fabric. In the recent decades, however, parts of the waterfront have been reconquered from these (often polluting) uses and developed as residential or mixed-use areas. At certain sites, nature has been restored and shorelines have been softened.

In this studio we would like to explore one element of these modern era developments that persist: New York City's coastal highways. The motivation behind such an exploration is based on three related issues:

1) Large stretches of the coastal highways will experience regular flooding by mid to late century

2) The locations of the coastal highways make them logical places for coastal protection systems

3) Many cities around the globe are re-thinking urban highways by either removing them, or by integrating them into the urban environment.

While many of New York's current resilience projects address those sections of highway that are part of the project, there is a lack of an overall vision on the future of these coastal highways. And while such a vision might be developed from a new perspective on the future traffic system, it would be greatly helped by exploring new architectural opportunities for the sites of the coastal highway, either after the highway's removal, or when integrated with the urban environment and/or flood protection. The limited amount of real estate available in New York City, as well as the potential of achieving multiple benefits, provide a strong incentive for exploring these.

The aim of this studio is to contribute to the conversation about the future of New York's coastal highways by developing speculative models and designs that re-imagine both the transportation system and the architectural challenges and opportunities such a re-imagination might bring.

Location: The Netherlands

HIGHWAYS TO RESILIENCE
Matthijs Bouw

Xiaoqing Meng, Calvin Vannoy

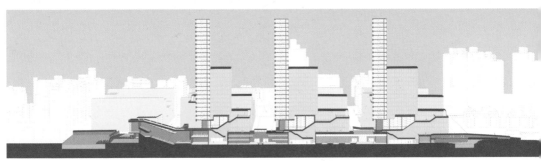

East Harlem, home to much of Manhattan's public housing, is largely in the floodzone. Removing the FDR drive by channeling the through traffic via Randall's Island and the Bronx creates space along its waterfront. The project proposes using this space for a new mixed-use development along the East River that includes replacement public housing. This development can trigger a transformation of East River Houses based on the principles of NYCHA 2.0, with a platform in which community functions and a local building industry are nested.

HIGHWAYS TO RESILIENCE
Matthijs Bouw

Riwan Heim, Shih-Kai Lin

In the future, large areas of the city will need to be given back to the sea. This means increased pressure on those areas that will be protected, such as Lower Manhattan. In order to accommodate this migration and facilitate climate adaptation there, land is added and big buildings are developed. This project is a prototype for one such building, on top of a newly designed Battery transit hub. The building is such that it is entirely public, with a framework that can be filled-in freely to accommodate the different communities who might migrate there.

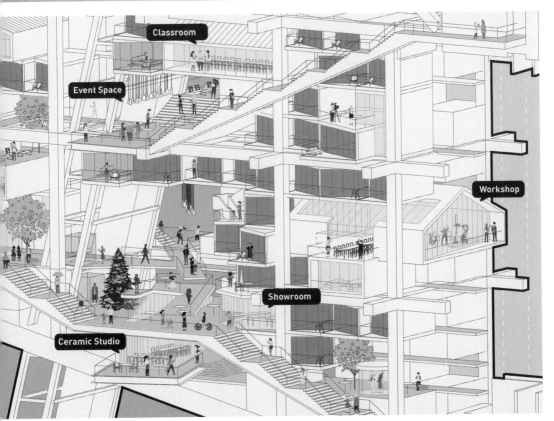

HACKING INFRASTRUCTURE: RADICAL HYBRIDS AS A STRATEGY FOR PUBLIC SPACE INFILL
Iñaki Echeverria
Stephen Rafferty (TA)

Architect and landscape urba[n]
based in Mexico City. Founder
of Iñaki Echeverria. The firm h[as]
been awarded numerous high
profile commissions, both pub[lic]
and private. Iñaki Echeverria
holds a M.Arch from the Grad[uate]
School of Architecture Plannin[g]
and Preservation at Columbia
University, a Bachelor's degre[e]
from UNAM in Mexico and Art
History studies at UCBerkeley

The studio will explore Hacking and/or Hybridization and/or Reconfiguring as an opportunity to integrate both architecture and mobility infrastructures while revising the city's possibilities to induce public space into the existing city fabric and the impact of this new typology.

This objective stems from a dramatic statistic: it is estimated that 65,000,000 km of paved roads exist today worldwide with an estimated cost of USD 70,000,000,000.

Also, according to the International Energy Agency (IEA), "Global road traffic activity is expected to more than double to nearly 43 trillion annual vehicle kilometers by 2050. To accommodate this growth, global road infrastructure is expected to increase by roughly 60% above 2010 levels by 2050."

Even so, road infrastructure has generally evolved little from a mono-functional paradigm. Unlike other forms of infrastructure, such as stormwater management, that have hybridized and become part of landscapes and/or cities, roads have resisted hybridization on many levels.

Our studio will explore the potential that lies in the possible hybridization of road infrastructure within the city fabric. Inspired by the evolution of other forms of infrastructure, such as the telephone, which went from single landlines to the portable powerhouses that we carry around today and allow far more than conversation. We will hack existing road infrastructure in the city and we will imagine futures where these spaces can do more for cities than allow motorized circulation.

We will redefine old typologies that have helped solve infrastructure/mobility problems in the past; analyze and collect data that will help shape an architectural project where transportation, social and environmental issues are resolved in a design methodology where architecture, landscape and public spaces converge; revise the spatial and environmental consequences that transforming the streetscape will have on the city's urban landscape, as well as revise how this solution responds to current global issues.

Our site of intervention is Reforma Avenue.

Mexico's most important corridor, symbolically and economically, is abruptly cut in two: a violent schism divides it into the rich west and poor east of the avenue. We will focus on "the poor" section and speculate on the potential for transformation of this space by hacking it and turning it multifunctional. In doing so, we will introduce much needed public space in the the neighborhoods around this area, and we will turn a space devoted to motorized mobility into a more complex construct with the capacity to introduce social, cultural and ecological agendas.

Location: Mexico City, Mexico

HACKING INFRASTRUCTURE: RADICAL HYBRIDS AS A STRATEGY FOR PUBLIC SPACE INFILL

Iñaki Echeverria

Caitlin Dashiell, Jinah Oh, Isabel Lopez-Font

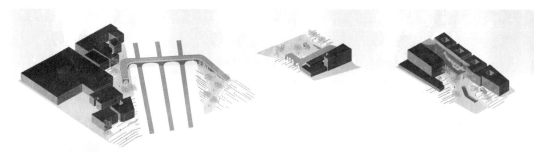

Changes in mobility will open up spaces within Mexico City where the odd, strange, and seemingly useless, now become sites for reconsideration for the future of urbanization. Bounded by La Reforma, Eje Central, and the Alameda, a patchwork of residential and vacant lots provide spaces for opportunity to reinvigorate this triangular site. This strategy implements a secondary infrastructure of redeveloped civic spaces through a tertiary pedestrian network that draws on the energy of La Reforma, Eje Central, Plaza Garibaldi, and Alamaeda, redistributing it within this neighborhood. The form was inspired by the prevalence of the arch in Mexican vernacular architecture, and its strength in a variety of configurations. By breaking down this form, iterations of the arc express the arch in various ways: subtracting from or adding to the existing infrastructure of the site. The resulting implementation explores combinations of our spatial and formal strategies to create a system of anchors and links.

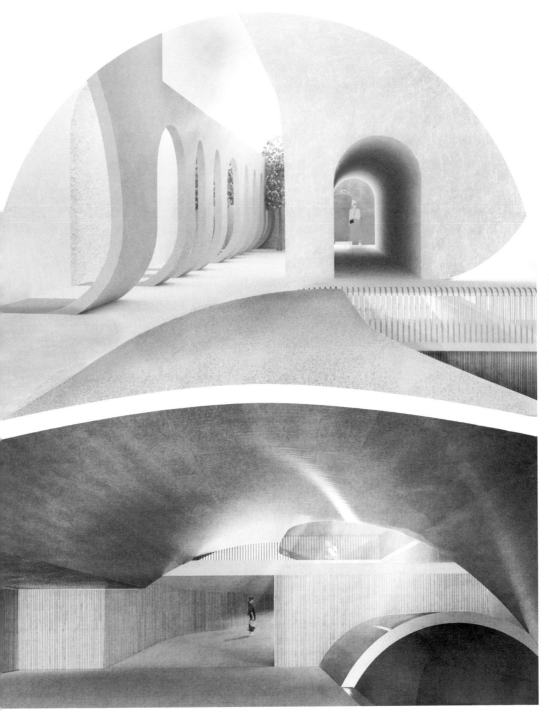

HACKING INFRASTRUCTURE: RADICAL HYBRIDS AS A STRATEGY FOR PUBLIC SPACE INFILL
Iñaki Echeverria

Xinyu Wang, Yefan Zhang

The la Reforma Avenue, with its dominant scale and diagonal relationship with its surroundings, is playing a very important role in terms of politics, culture and publicity in the Mexico City. But now, its main function is transportation. The width of the street is so big that it makes it difficult for pedestrians to cross with ease, and therefore its publicity and accessibility has been weakened. Could streets have multi-functions other than transportation, and what could it have? This is the question we have always been asking since the beginning of this project. In this way, we are trying to amplify the three possibilities on this street, to make it not only a space for mobility, but also a political statement of the people, a cultural center of Mexico, and a public space for citizens.

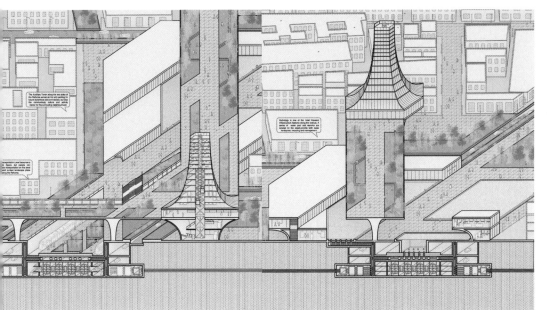

CRITIC: HOMA FARJADI

HOUSE OF TOMORROW
Homa Farjadi
Pierandrea Angius (TA)

Homa Farjadi (M.Arch, RIBA, AF
is Principal of Farjadi architects i
London and Professsor in Pract
of Architecture at the Universit
of Pennsylvania where she also
responsible for the teaching of tl
London Studio at the Architectu
Association, London.
She has been a unit master
the AA School of Architecture
1980-88, associate professor o
arch GSD Harvard University
1989-96 and has held chaired visit
professorships at Yale, UPenn
and Edinburgh universities as w
as visiting professorships at
Columbia university and Univer
sity of Virginia in the US, and
Karlsruhe University in German
The work of her office has be
exhibited at MOMA New York,
Barcelona, Walker Artcente, Vien
Tokyo, Beijing, etc.

Monographs:
Delayed space 1993
Sense geometries 2014

Her projects have received
numerous prizes in internationa
design competitions and awards
of distinction for built work

This studio poses the design of a house/ houses for a near future in the UK. In framing styles of living, in constructing versions of community and gradations of public and private domains, design of houses have, in their intersection with other geographic and programmatic formulation of work, leisure and life, can be said to have historically set up primary criteria for scaling spaces of domestic life as well as structural formation of cities.

In our project it is to be treated as a speculative encounter between its modernist past as analyzed in the text by Inaki Abalos and speculations on the near future of the house inspired by Smithson's design in the context of the UK.

Inaki Abalos' text visits seven houses of modernity to describe how ideas and ways of thinking about good life in each intersects with formation of space of the house, planning and living in it not as manuals for forms of domestic architecture but a map of the crossing of the two modes of thinking.

The positions offered take up a range. In Mies Van der Rohe's patio houses where "the grouping of consistently different units, deliberately and clearly individualized by topological devices, a different positioning of the house, different proportion of the plot, different depth and orientation, or metric ones, greater or lesser size of the plot, greater or lesser size of the house." The idea of individualizing a "system" that is operating with a small number of interconnected variables so as to arrive at a perfect and varied result; be it constructional, spatial or structural. Another example examines Jacque Tati's machine for living in which he enacts with critical humor what Abalos calls a Positivist house and as a model for order and technological progress formulated by the modernist obsession with progress, hygenic obsession and corporeality of its Cartesian res extensa in early modernism. Yet another protagonist is formulated by the life lived in the Warhol Factory as the Freudo Marxist commune at the origin of the New York Loft. Later we are confronted with the parasites and nomads deconstructing life in the house or the house of pragmatism which he presents through the case study houses. In each we are invited to examine ideas around the role of ordered design, ad-hoc materiality, sentimental objects, intimacy, architect as bricoleur, living in an urban commune, on vacation, or in various degrees of intensity of belonging within the existential house.

The Smithsons' example is an exercise in rethinking anthropology of the 20 c house in relation to its mediatic role, its technologies of quircky prefabrication and prefigures an anthropology of life as a show.

Studio Hosted at the Architectural Association School of Architecture in London (the AA)

HOUSE OF TOMORROW
Homa Farjadi

Justine Huang, Keaton Kane

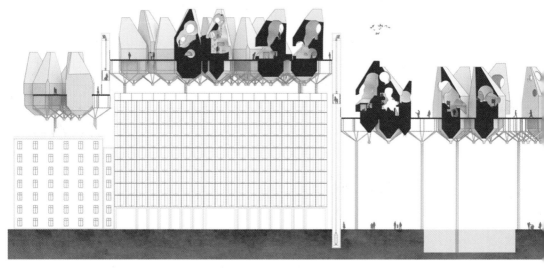

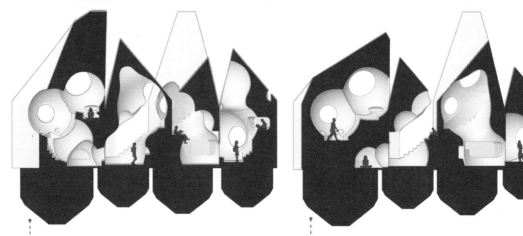

In approaching our vision for the house of the future, we were interested in looking at the subject of the nomad and the future of extreme consumerism. We have envisioned a house of temporality that exists in line with the ever changing and transient culture of nomadism. To facilitate this planned obsolescence, we have utilized the technology of 3D printing in combination with the impermanence of salt. As a vehicle for consumerist waste, we foresee the nomad's desire to dispose of their homes post-use and have therefore chosen this material for its dissolvable qualities. To further facilitate the nomad's need for change and individuality, the houses are designed to be carved into in order to mold the space to their needs and desires. Additionally, we have chosen to focus on the idea of exhibitionism and the celebration of everyday life by inviting the public to traverse the landscape of this housing project through a series of pathways that offer views into the houses. We envision this network of nomadic life proliferating throughout the whole of London via existing waterways.

HOUSE OF TOMORROW
Homa Farjadi

Mohamed Ali, Cheuk Wai Lam, Yi Zhu

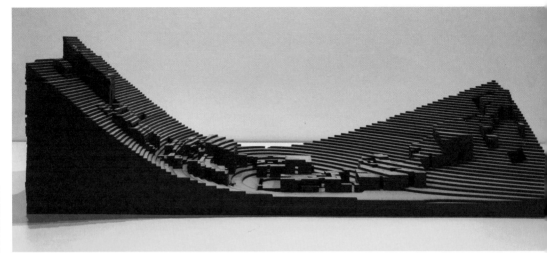

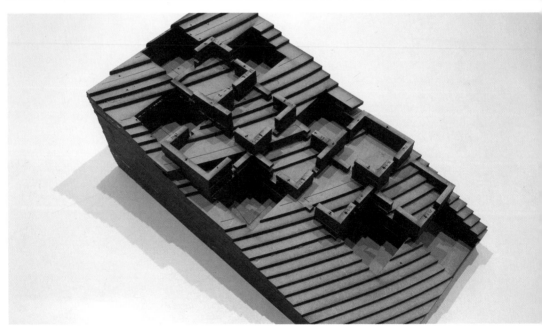

The Natures Project explores the discourse of people and nature through a speculation of living in 30 years. In Iñaki Ábalos' book, *The Good Life*, Heidegger's Hut was introduced as the prototype for a lifestyle in friction with progressive technology. Arguing against the incessant onslaught of progressive technology, Heidegger's retreat was one about centering and living. Living in the form of inhabiting, to inhabit is to live. From the idea of inhabiting and paralleling that with Smithson's House of the Future, a futurist speculation house towards the '80s, The Natures Project establishes an ongoing relationship between the "primordial nature" and the digital "nature" in which we inhabit. It is a project about inhabiting. A project which debates the conditions of what we presume to be nature and the "nature" we reside in the digital age.

WHITE WASH AND THE ESSENTIAL AESTHETICS OF MASS
Georgina Huljich
Miguel Abaunza (TA)

M.Arch., UC Los Angeles, Diplo
National University of Rosario
Assistant Adjunct Professor, UC
Principal and Managing Directo
of P-A-T-T-E-R-N-S (Los Ange
CA), AIA/LA Next Design Awar
(AFH Office Building, 2017), A
LA Next Design Award (Victor
Healthcare, 2016), First Prize
Arc Graduation Pavilion (2012
United States Artist Fellowsh
(2012), 2005-2006 Maybeck Fe
at UC Berkeley

CRITIC: GEORGINA HULJICH

"In their crazy course, red, blue, and yellow have become white. I am crazy about the color white, the cube, the sphere, the cylinder, and the pyramid and the disc all united and the great empty expanse. The white of the white-wash is absolute, everything stands out from it and is recorded absolutely, black on white; it is honest and dependable" -Le Corbusier

As urban developments in cities across the globe grow at a rate never seen before throughout history, our discipline seems to have failed to produce any underlying theory which could grapple with that which is decidedly not urban. Known as "the rural" or countryside, these areas are characterized for low density, low population, and small settlements.

Furthermore, the notion of island or "islandness" [while slightly different than that of the rural through its insularity and remoteness] implies a literal territorial and geographic disconnection from the mainland, from its culture and identity.

Remote islands particularly depend on external markets; present high costs for energy, infrastructure, transportation, communication and ser-vicing; long distances from export markets and import resources; low and irregular international Unslaked Lime Island Village near Ayorou, Niger, Africa traffic volumes; little resilience to natural disasters; growing populations; high volatility of economic growth; a proportionately large reliance of their economies on their public sector; and fragile natural environments.

In the early 1920s, Le Corbusier visited Greece; specifically the Cyclades Islands. It is not necessary to convey the fact that the classical architecture of Greece would have an extraordinary influence on his subsequent work, as well as the vernacular style of islands like Mykonos and Santorini. Moreover, he later stated: "Unless you have seen the houses of Mykonos, you cannot pretend to be an architect, whatever architecture had to say, it is said here." His passion for their plasticity, their wisdom of anonymous architecture and whitewashed vernacular was to become his pure expression of Modernism.

The studio intends to propose paradigms for island development and growth that incorporates architecture, landscape, and territory as a form of "second nature," a man-made ecology able to be at the same time integrated with its larger geography yet relatively autonomous and self-sufficient from it. We will work on a "rural ensemble," consisting of a grouping of both existing and new buildings on a large rural terrain. The class will explore the construction of architecture not just as a formal whole, but as a figural patchwork wherein disparate and yet conforming styles, buildings and volumes will coexist, strangely.

How can we produce a project wherein character is no longer purely historic? How to create extravagance through modesty and muteness?

Using abstract and de-familiarizing techniques to instigate infractions on, and misappropriations of the real, the studio will aim to propose a new archi-tectural paradigm for the rural outskirts: one that is comfortably at odds with its context and "whitewashed" vernacular references as a foundation for its originality. Rather than falling into known functional paradigms of repetition and standardization, the studio will attempt to inventively combine advanced approaches to form, plasticity and materiality with notions of local traditions and use of available craftsmanship in a creative way.

Studio Sponsor: Karma Group and John Spence
Location: Athens and Mykonos, Greece

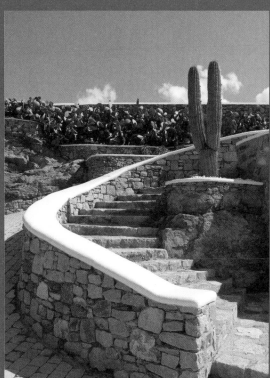

WHITE WASH AND THE ESSENTIAL AESTHETICS OF MASS
Georgina Huljich

Alexandra Adamski, Logan Weaver

"Anchorage" is a proposal for a resort in Mykonos, Greece that engages with architectural questions of autonomy, tectonics, fiction, and the vernacular. The resort exists as a composition of built farms that push and pull at the seams and edges of the natural terrain of Mykonos.

Historically, Mykonian architecture has followed its environment. Its circulation is terraced and fragmented by topographic shifts, its buildings are cloistered and embrace solidity to respond to strong winds and sun.

"Anchorage" respects these traditional, intuitive strategies, while creating a more nuanced dialogue between architecture and site. Its buildings are deeply embedded in the terrain, taking on an anchored quality that suggests a more permanent and aged relationship with the ubiquitous Mykonian bedrock. Simultaneously, the terrain embeds itself in the architecture. Walls and ceilings are covered with layers of thick, informal stone, rusticating their otherwise smooth texture. Rocks, earth, and vegetation overtake circulatory branches, creating paths that lack clear termini. The buildings' masses are formed through tactics of removal, privileging exterior spaces and views, while withdrawing and simplifying the experience of the interior.

These formal methods and spatial relationships help to shape the human experience of the resort. Visitors are encouraged to explore the project's meandering paths, leisurely discovering a myriad of public spaces that manifest at scales ranging from pools and dance floors to alcoves designed for those seeking a moment of contemplation.

As the name suggests, "Anchorage" attempts to create a resort experience that is rooted in social, conceptual, and architectural traditions, while giving appropriate attention to the notion that a holistic experience of Mykonos necessarily includes complex intersections of built and unbuilt, historic and new, vernacular and autonomous.

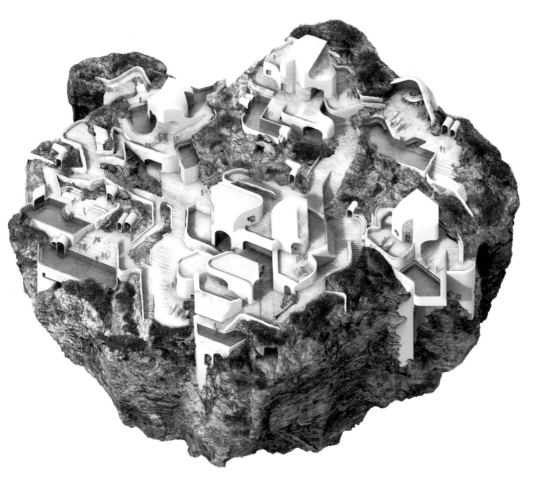

WHITE WASH AND THE ESSENTIAL AESTHETICS OF MASS
Georgina Huljich

Andrew Matia, Daniel Silverman

CRITIC: GEORGINA HULJICH

When considering the architectural mass of Meteora we realized there is no such thing as singular essences but rather dichotomies, whether material, atmospheric or tectonic. Thus we became intrigued by forms that flicker between various readings created by their silhouette; something we discovered in our contextual research. For us, the ambiguity of whitewash, a medium that is both negator and enhancer, is one that allows the essential aesthetic of pure mass to emerge for a multiplicities of essences to exist in the same architecture. For example, the mass of Meteora appears impenetrable from the vantage point of an underbelly who's horizon often ends in a flat wall. This is useful to concentrate ones focus on the activity taking place in these spaces, whether it is eating at a communal table or participating in morning yoga. On the other hand, the view from the central corridor appears quite porous, inviting gazes and engagement Ultimately, our goal was to use the wall, whether literal or representative, as the interface for architectural intervention.

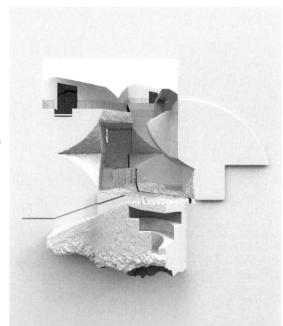

MONTREAL, SENSATE AND AUGMENTED
Simon Kim
Brett Lee (TA)

Co-founded Ibañez Kim Studio, PA & MA, (1994). Graduated fr the Design Research Laborato at the Architectural Associatic (AA). Taught studios and seminars at Harvard, MIT, Yale, and the AA. Director of the Immers Kinematics Research Group

The architecture of a city—as a proposition or a form of intellectual investigation —is tethered to an enveloping, shared environment. Its implicit and explicit meanings and effects are to be developed in material, atmospherics, ecologies, and also in behavior over time.

To do this, we will imbue architecture and urbanism with duration, with its own agency and self-governance in what was the site for Expo '67, in Montreal. With new media and new materials, it is not impossible to revisit this iconic project and conceptualize the built environment as a sensate and sentient field of beings. Our role as designers and as inhabitants is to coordinate and live in this new city and new nature as a shared endeavor. Montreal's history of Expos and Olympics places it as an ideal post-industrial model with an aim towards advanced thinking of synthetic-environment and eco-intelligence.

This studio will break from the classical hierarchy of human-centric design and allow for nonhuman (all manner of flora, fauna, and matter) to have authorship and stewardship. Rather than design from a compositional position, and to dwell in a seamless zone of human comfort, this studio will engage in a design process with transformations over time, to produce environments that change and behave for other-than-human criteria (such as the seasons, water, temperature, animal).

We will consider the postwar projects of Gordon Pask, Nicholas Negroponte, and the writings of Timothy Morton and Gilbert Simondon, while rejecting the mecca-ideologies of Metabolism and Evangelion. Architecture that is sensate and nervous do not need to look like giant robots, and projects based in Canada should not be simplified to an easy reading or cliche (i.e. winter and the lumber industry).

Location: Montreal, Canada

MONTREAL, SENSATE AND AUGMENTED
Simon Kim

Mostafa Akbari, Wenqi Huang

The mechanism is to simulate the transition from the artificial process to the natural self-growing system. The essence about the evolution is to annihilate and regenerate. The architecture starts from the half-machine core, applying similar method like hydroponics, which is to incessantly collect nutrition from the nearby soil, lake and air, then classify and transmit those materials to the different parts of roots and branches. Since the substances in the surrounding environment have been changed, the atmosphere would be altered as well.

After hundreds of years and consistently growing, the roots and branches twine with the building and become an entity at the end of the day. The tree is already part of the shell and we can't tell the clear boundary between the life and dead nor can't tell whether the root is transformed from plant to petrified wood and finally integrate with the rock, or the rock have also been changed and have life elements within it.

Same thing in terms of the different materiality and transformation process. Where do roots stop and the human biome begin to grow? What if the human/ Plants can sense from the surroundings with totally different organs? The roots can evolve into humidity attractor or solar panels, the new life can also be born from the transformation between organic and non-organic.

MONTREAL, SENSATE AND AUGMENTED
Simon Kim

Zihao Fang, Bowen Qin, Weimeng Zhang

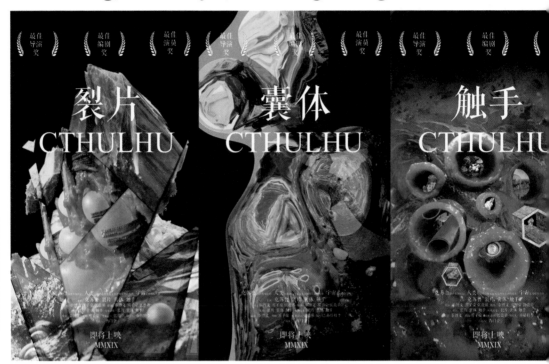

The concept of Cthulhu comes from the concept of Cthulhu Mythos, which was created for Howard Phillips Lovecraft in 1928 and has influenced many works since then. The core of Cthulhu's world is that the limited human mind can never understand the nature of life, and the universe is cruel and strange to us.

As a creature, though most of the time it is regarded as evil, Cthulhu has always been the spokesman of the natural world, the existence of inseparable good and evil.

On Montreal's deserted island after the cold war, a new world slowly occurs. It started with a combination of organisms contaminated by nuclear chemistry, aquatic thylakoids, terrestrial crustaceans and amphibious coral-like life that grew up absorbing the basic elements of the environment and, by chance, had the initial intelligence.

As evolution proceeds, the three individuals become more and more sensitive to each other. For the purpose of better survival, they naturally proceed to the next step: integration.

After the assembly, the demand of the self-evolution and replication drastically increased its demand for resources. The Cthulhu begin to transform environment to a new world that can continues provide resources. This process is surprisingly like the birth of agriculture in human society.

In the final step, the newly born Cthulhu individuals begin to integrate into the natural environment. The result is that it successfully disguises itself in the environment. Also, the nature itself becomes its extension. The earth begins to breathe. The coral like structure begins to absorb resources. New life feeding in the cysts. A new world which was entirely different from the human world was formed.

克苏鲁
CTHULHU

即将上映
MMXIX

ODDKIN ARCHITECTURE
TOPHANE – GALATAPORT, ISTANBUL
Ferda Kolatan
Michael Zimmerman (TA)

Founding Director of SU11 Architecture+Design, MsAAD, Columbia University, Dipl.Ing., RWTH Aachen, German

CRITIC: FERDA KOLATAN

ODDKIN: *Beings (and things) requiring each other in unexpected collaborations and combinations. Being situated someplace and not noplace, entangled and worldly.* - Donna Haraway, *Staying with the Trouble* (2016)

Donna Haraway's recent coinage of the word "oddkin" delivers an intriguing recalibration of how we view the things around us. Turning away from predetermined categories with their strict hierarchies, Haraway directs our attention toward odd couplings and hybrids as the real constituents of our contemporary world. "Making kin" across types, categories, and species challenges our long western tradition of viewing the world through a privileged anthropocentric lens with little regard for both nonhumans as well as any kind of categorical ambiguity.

While Haraway's writing is mostly directed toward new concepts of nature and ecology, it is also very useful as a speculative tool for architecture. This is the case not only because architecture deals with nature and ecology, but also because of our own complicity in creating the anthropocentric paradigm, which has now become so out of sync with the actual circumstances of our day. At the eve of the Fourth Industrial Revolution -populated by oddkins and hybrids- architecture needs to revise its own anachronistic paradigms and articulate new concepts and strategies that adequately reflect our current situation.

This studio aimed to develop "oddkin" design strategies for architecture in the city. Cities—being conglomerations of vastly different objects and agencies—are perfect testing grounds for oddkin constellations. And yet, we rarely seem to acknowledge this fact in the way we design, preferring instead to streamline existing diversities into homogenous and abstract expressions of unity. By doing so we necessarily fall back into category-thinking of old and new, special and mundane, useful and useless, and so forth. Our Oddkin Architecture Istanbul Studio rejects any such polarities and views all material expressions of a city as equally valuable in their potential to create novel hybrid qualities for the city.

The Tophane neighborhood in Istanbul was chosen as a site because it is already populated with odd diversities such as historical landmarks, infrastructural elements, green spaces, as well as institutional, cultural, and commercial programs. The students were asked to embrace the idiosyncratic qualities of this place and to design new urban objects by locating unlikely affinities across time and type. These urban objects, while serving specific functions, are primarily an attempt to articulate a new kind of urbanism, which neither overrides the existing qualities with sweeping, modernist schemes, nor falls back into historicism or regionalism. Our oddkin architecture combines in unfamiliar ways image, ornament, pattern, type, and tectonics into new coherent wholes, which cannot be disassociated from the place and yet produce uniquely contemporary results.

Studio Sponsor: GAD Foundation of Istanbul, Turkey
Location: Istanbul, Turkey

ODDKIN ARCHITECTURE
TOPHANE – GALATAPORT, ISTANBUL
Ferda Kolatan

Carla Bonilla, Yang Li, Neera Sharma

This project weaves between the interstitial and the urban in order to deal with a non-site, playing with existing strange characteristics to create new hybrids. Located at one of the major intersections of the Tophane quarter, this project connects to the existing Tophane building and its terraces to create an art gallery and tram station.

The interstitial deals with the oddities located on the façade of the Tophane I-amire building, locating itself within the thickness of the wall. It creates a new reading of the existing elements on the facade, reframing an oddly-positioned and abandoned baroque door, and re-purposing its deserted large basement entrances. It uses these elements to create narrow spaces carving into the ground and generating an art gallery in the in-betweens.

The tram station on the other side positions itself as a connector, creating a bridge between Tophane's terraces and the park on the other side of the street. It uses the Dolmabahce Palace's crystal stairs as a starting point, hybridizing with the bridge and platform to create a semi-enclosed space. Within this semi-interior, Tophane motifs re-appear, merging themselves with an Ebru pattern. This pattern creates ambiguity between itself and the form of the space, as well as physicalizes in handrails, lighting elements, and ticket machines.

ODDKIN ARCHITECTURE
TOPHANE – GALATAPORT, ISTANBUL
Ferda Kolatan

Wenjia Guo, Yuanyi Zhou

CRITIC: FERDA KOLATAN

Our project for a new Sanatkarlar Park in Istanbul aims to hybridize things
found within the city in order to make a new site that will attract people
from the port area and exhibit the mixing of traditional and modern Turkish
aesthetics that are uniquely found within the city. The project explores
different ways to produce natural, architectural, and urban spaces by hybridizing things like muqarna and stair details, handrails and infrastructural
elements, and most importantly carving techniques. About half of the site is
built up and paved as cavernous architectural spaces, and the other half of
the site is left to be excavated by large trucks and then refined and polished
by robotic arms. These new landscapes are places for interaction between
human, natural, and machine aesthetics. From faraway, the park merges with
the surrounding trees and landscape, but when people get closer they will
find strange relationships and exciting experiences of colors and materials.
Bright and colorful patterns mark the stairs and other architectural
features and simultaneously bleed into the patterning of plants and other
natural features within the park. An observant user may notice additional
hybridized objects like water pipes, handrails, and lights, while the unknowing
passerby will still be enchanted by this strange new park.

SUSTAINABLE EVOLUTIONS: EXPO 2020 DUBAI AND THE SUSTAINABILITY PAVILION
Joe MacDonald
Zachary Kile (TA)

M.Arch Harvard, B.Arch Univ
of Washington, Urban A&O, ID
International Design Excellence
Award for Environments for
the Water Planet, China's Mo
Successful Design Award for
the Johnson & Johnson Olym
Pavilion in Beijing, Architectur
Magazine's Vanguard Award, I
Practices New York from the
New York Chapter of the AIA,
Design Award, Archi-tech AV
Award for the Water Planet, L
Gold recognition award for
Johnson & Johnson Olympic Pa
in Beijing, LEED Platinum
Recognition for Water Planet

Our project reexamines the Sustainability Pavilion and near-future strategies for sustainable practice and living. Our designs promise to deliver new definitions of intelligent occupancy and experience both within the building enclosure and in the urban territory beyond. The skin itself becomes the site of inquiry as we investigate innovations in breathing materiality. With the Sustainability Pavilion as our subject, this studio will explore strategies that redefine contemporary definitions of sustainability as we imagine new building assemblies and materiality for architecture in a future that you are invited to research and imagine.

Students will learn the need for energy-efficient, radically better, sustainable architectures by means of sustained research found in both academia and in practice. We must think of our work as focused in integrated systems of sustainability. Research underway that we can access includes day-lighting systems, energy harvesting, air filtration, manufacturing technologies and composite materials. All contribute to a definition of what a resilient city might be.

In the 1970s, James Lovelock and Lynn Margulis formed a hypothesis that life on earth regulates its own environment. They posited that there is an interaction between living organisms and their inorganic host to form a synergistic, self-regulating system that maintains the conditions for life on earth. It is a theory that has always been questioned, but there is greater and greater reason for us to look into Gaia again given the rapidly changing ecologies on earth. The Gaia hypothesis focuses on observing how the biosphere and the evolution of life forms contribute to the stability of global temperature, ocean salinity and oxygen in the atmosphere.

In tandem with the Gaia hypothesis, Biophilic Design offers a strategy for the role of plant life in contributing to health and productivity, and becomes a formal device and a building material both inside and outside the building envelope.

Location: Dubai and Masdar City, UAE

SUSTAINABLE EVOLUTIONS: EXPO 2020 DUBAI AND THE SUSTAINABILITY PAVILION

Joe MacDonald

Jongwon Lee, Zehua Qi, Xieyang Zhou

Sandstock pavilion, based on Masdar Institute research from United Arab Emirates, projects 2050's potential of integrating sand and solar technology to operate a self-sustaining system. The architecture suggests a system in which sand particle movements are curated to become expo exhibitions with various scale and representations, as well as the audiences witness the energy transformations with sand. Along Opportunity pavilion and Mobility pavilion, our project as Sustainability pavilion will be the epitome of how the energy production process could also be aesthetic and articulate to make future further rich and dynamic.

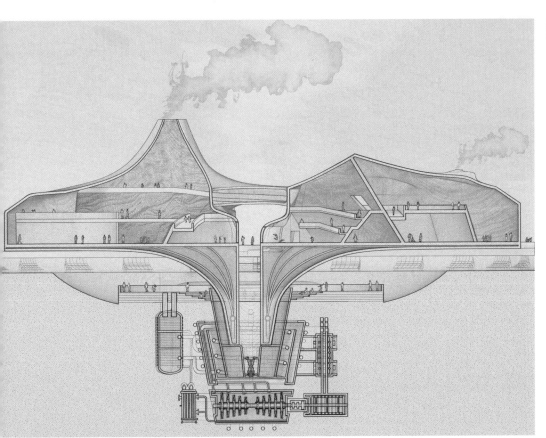

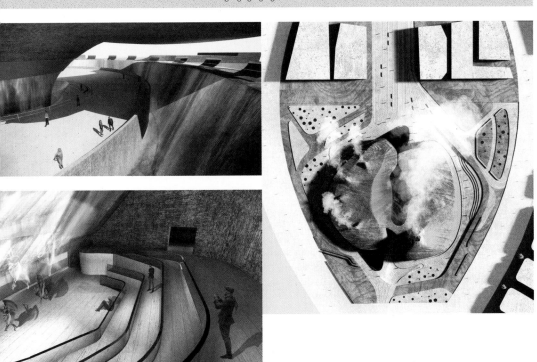

SUSTAINABLE EVOLUTIONS:
EXPO 2020 DUBAI AND
THE SUSTAINABILITY PAVILION

Joe MacDonald

Xu Yao, Long Ye

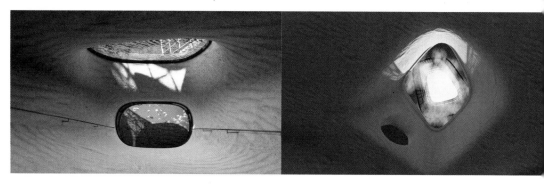

The museum is designed on the foundation of sand as the building material on site as well as the nature of the climate. The juxtaposition of the museum orients itself to outlook the development of the expo as well as the natural sand dunes in the far horizon. Three-dimensional printing using local sand as the construction method and material, the project emphasizes the contrast between nature and technology, more importantly, how we could utilize technology in minimizing carbon footprint in constructions. The secondary skin on the surface of the building is a layer of wire mesh woven by metal pipes that form structural and functional integrity. The wire mesh is to collect and condense the humidity of the water in the air, and the tube is the irrigation system. The water continually travels through the pipe and into the ground to maintain a cold temperature, during the day, water is sprayed into the openings of the building to create mists that cool the building down. The building digs deep below ground to reach cooler temperature, thus allowing a sustainable conditioned space during the harsh heat in the day.

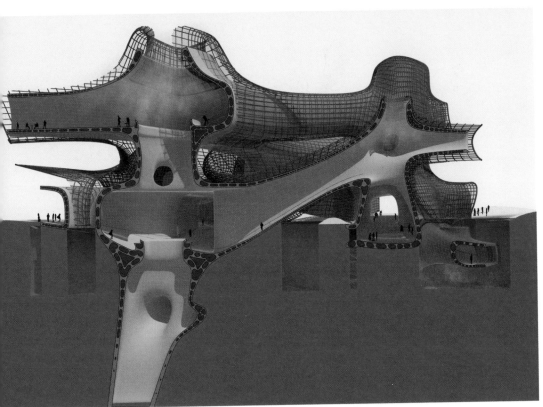

COMBINATORY CAMPUS TENCENT "INTERNET+" FUTURE SCI-TECH CITY
Thom Mayne
Trudy Watt (TA)

Founding Principal + Design Director, Morphosis, Cret Cha Professor of Practice, Weitzm School, Pritzker Prize (2005), AIA Gold Medal (2013), Bachelo of Architecture, University of Southern California (1968), Master of Architecture, Harvard University Graduate School of Design (1978)

CRITIC: THOM MAYNE

As architects, it is vital to understand the city as an evolving organism, an open-ended design that contrasts markedly with the closed-end assemblage that is associated with architecture. So how does one design for an open-ended ecology where the evolution is not authored or predicted at every detail? Combinatory Urbanism offers an alternative method of urban production that designs flexible frameworks of relational systems within which activities, events, and programs can organically play themselves out. As such, Combinatory Urbanism, engages the premise of continuous process over static form, identifying the socio-political imperatives of architecture while pushing formal organizational possibilities.

Located on an extraordinary site on the western end of Shenzhen, Tencent "Internet+" Future Sci-Tech City is a rare opportunity to examine the premises of Combinatory Urbanism. What the Tencent "Internet+" Future Sci-Tech City will become depend largely on its ability to establish its own planning raison d'etre through the interrogation of diverse development strategies that are translated into operational, programmatic and cultural systems.

Tencent is the world's fifth largest technology company and China's second largest after Alibaba. As a compa-ny, Tencent represents the aspiration and the potential of technology to shape the future of Chinese economy, social infrastructure, global relevance and technological leadership.

The site strategy lies in organizing these operational and programmatic systems that are spatial, physical and flexible. As well-integrated and sustainable set of systems and develop an inherent intelligence that adapts, optimizes, and allows for multiple unseen elements, narratives, desires, contamination and lives. These systems, in turn, are integrated to produce a relationship between architecture and urbanism that is acutely intimate and inseparable; infrastructure, housing, social values, service-manufacturing economies and politics co-mingle to create a complex organism within a hyper-heterogenous ecosystem. These interwoven urban systems are critical to your ability site architecture in a way where it maximizes the architecture's relevance and potential and ultimately advances urban life.

Location: Los Angeles, CA

COMBINATORY CAMPUS TENCENT "INTERNET+" FUTURE SCI-TECH CITY
Thom Mayne

Nicole Bronola, Jordan Hillier, Ayotunde Ogunmoyero, Grace Soejanto

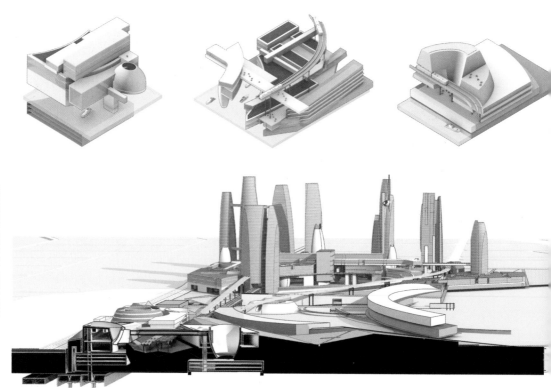

Located in Shenzhen, one of the fastest growing cities in China, this project maneuvers the dichotomy between revolutionary and nostalgic. Dissecting the nature of company towns in the 21st century, A Tale of Two Cities aims to address the metamorphic relationship between working and living. Designed as a new headquarters for the one of the world's leading tech companies, Tencent, A Tale of Two Cities offers a unique approach to the programmatic desires to create a space in which staff can both live and work. Shying away from the relatively normative approach of interweaving the two, this project creates two distinct campuses located on either end of the 2.5-km-long site; one for working and one for living. Both campuses are differentiated by a series of "rules" that physical distinguish the two from one another. The high-density "City Campus," where 85% of Tencent's work takes place, sits entirely on water and is divided by a grid, pulled from the surrounding city of Shenzhen, that is composed of an immense structure of plinths and towers. The low-density "Island Campus" rests at the other end of the site and houses all the residential structures. These two districts perform as a cohesive mass because of the immense transportation infrastructure that connects them underneath and the "Green Link."

   In attempts to reaffirm Shenzhen's efforts to bring greenery to the waterfront, the Green Link was added as a large, green-filled, connective tissue that ties the living and working districts to one another, as well as to the rest of Shenzhen. Connecting the Tencent site to the James Corner Field Operations "Water City," the Green Link gives occupants of the site the option to interact with the new landscape, rather than admire it from across the water.

CIAL PROGRAMS

CENTER
FACILITIES
UNITY CENTER
GATHERING
PACE

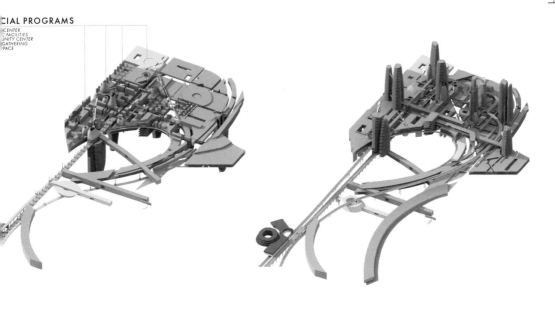

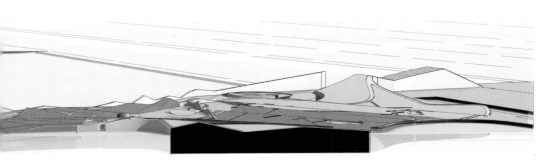

COMBINATORY CAMPUS TENCENT "INTERNET+" FUTURE SCI-TECH CITY
Thom Mayne

Xuanhao Han, Bingyu Wang, Yitian Zheng

CRITIC: THOM MAYNE

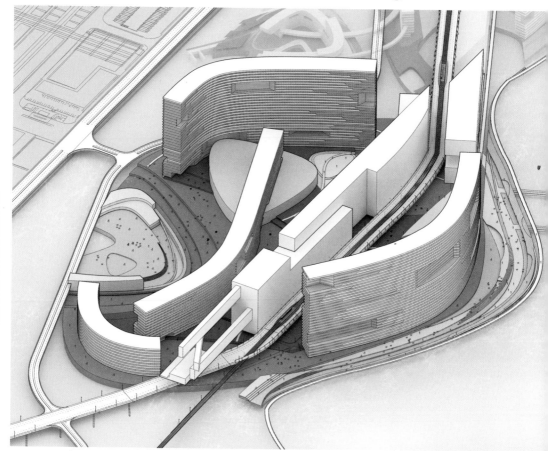

Tencent has become a growing tech giant in China, businesses covering gaming platform to online social media. Tencent headquarter in Shenzhen has asked the design team to propose a new campus for their employees and to provide a new way of balancing work and life. Seeing the homogeneity of program arrangements within the existing Shenzhen city blocks, our team is proposing a heterogenous way of living where work and life are combined into one place. The whole site is divided into seven islands, in response to the division of departments within the Tencent corporate firm. The seven islands create seven distinct campuses which dedicate to different programs. The R&D, which is the research and development department becomes the connecting tissue that links the islands together, making them separate as well as attach. Our urban strategy is to separate site into public, semi-public, and private landscapes with the public one sitting on the right side, extending all the way through the seven islands, providing public space for walking. Semi-public parks and private parks are located within each island, providing outdoor experiences that midiate between living and working. Ecologically, the interstitial space created by the seven islands, along with the waterfront landscape proposed by James Corner's Field Operation, becomes a water remediation system to filter out water that's been polluted. The whole north end of the site is wetland, which is dedicated to purifying water which has the slowest flow rate.

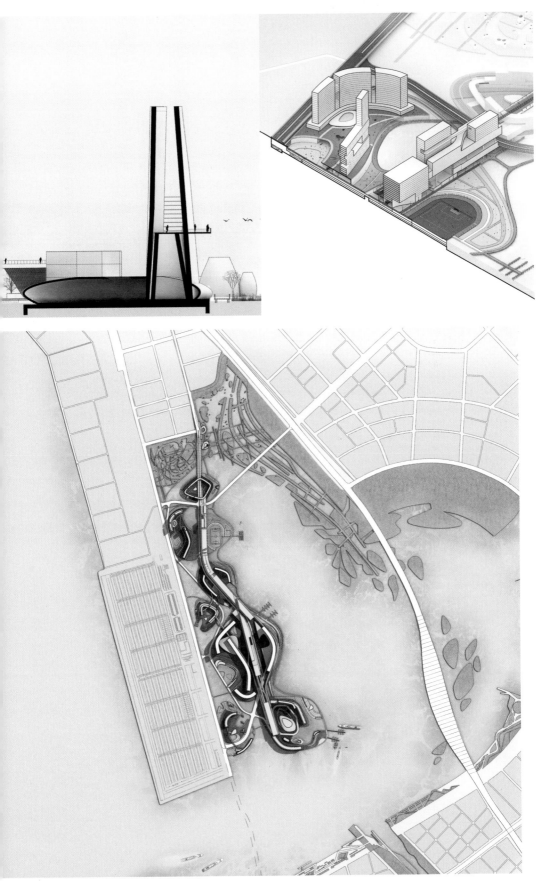

DIRT AND ROCKS AND MAYBE LOGS AND THINGS
Paul Preissner
Caroline Morgan (TA)

Founding partner of Paul or Paul. AIA studied architectur at the University of Illinois (B.Arch) and Columbia Univer (M.Arch). He has has taught at the University of Pennsylva Syracuse University, the Southern California Institute of Architecture

The history of modernity is the history of democracies, and this history of democracies is the history of the Public Hall, which exists as possibly the most confused of all contemporary programs; physically lost, both intended to soften interactions and formalize them.

The hall is the truly inauthentic program in today's world, unable to be anything else but a host to communal social space, collective experience and unpracticed democracy. It is an embassy of expectation within the urban space; always populated by locals.

The design for a new Public Hall using unadulterated excavated materials offers a unique opportunity to us. This population of weary residents, recreating foreigners and goal-driven transients opens a world of confusing social space, transactions and negotiations which needs a proper home.

In order to properly consider the demands of democracy's maintenance, we will look back to the earth—deep into the earth—to the minerals and materials which provide us the crudest and dumbest ways to fortify ambition and support a roof: rocks. Our Halls will be a solid as the nature of its internal business is shaky.

Consider the possibility of a world where buildings have never existed; a place ignorant to the single-family home or the shiny steel skyscraper. Here there has never been the concept of classicism nor modernism. There is no idea of what an office or a subdivision or a museum should be. How could we design an architecture if anything was possible and nothing had been established as conventional construction? Rocks are not things to be cut and polished into clean dimensions. Piles of gravel and dirt are meant to be used in the current configurations. Crude stacks of heavy, unavoidably present mass gives on height, while slabs have no way to hide their horizontal heaviness, and present as irregular platforms. In order to reinvent the notion of architecture, this studio will look to advance the nature of compositional arrangements without the facility of engineered materials, structures, frames and other ways to make architecture look less than its parts. And what to make of stairs and doors and other functional objects of the building with no clear way to integrate them into the construction (what is a stair to a boulder, or an elevator to a massive pile of crushed limestone?).

Location: St. John's, Newfoundland, Canada

DIRT AND ROCKS AND MAYBE LOGS AND THINGS

Paul Preissner

Katie Lanski

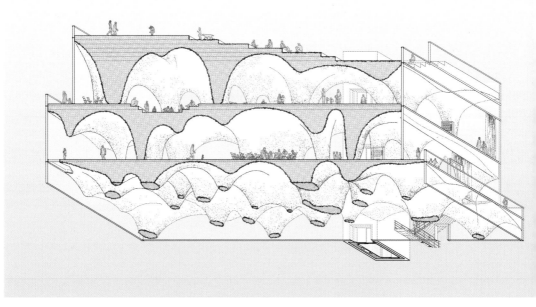

Built upon a combination of wet sand, wet sod, and sometimes boulders, the cast-in-place concrete of the Newfoundland Public Hall provides diverse spatial, textural, and atmospheric experiences for the visitor. Two rock-, boulder-, and grass-filled plazas welcome the visitor to sit, climb, picnic, heckle, or enter the building. Ranging from intimate hidey-hole to expansive vault, the Public Hall provides moments of serenity for individuals and vending machines, meeting rooms for friends, bingo nights for community members, hide-and-seek for children, movie screenings for film enthusiasts, and forum spaces for local artists and storytellers.

The interior space of the Public Hall is designed through strategic additive and subtractive methods. The additive method harvests the material intelligence of sand and sod through pouring, as each material acts as a liquid until hardened with an application of water, followed by concrete. These material pours produce medium to large gathering spaces. The subtractive method acts as a carving away of the wet sand and wet sod, followed by the pouring of concrete to produce smaller, more intimate moments. The stepped-forum space acts in the opposite way; concrete is poured first, the sand and sod are poured second, pushing the concrete outward and upward in the production of stepped moments. Through these methods, the materials create varied atmospheres: dark and rough walls produced by the large-grained sod, light and sandpaper-like walls produced by the finer grained sand, varied colorations and surface textures produced by a mixture of these two.

Roughly formed apertures in the floors reflect the residue of the construction process used while providing light, sneak peaks to above and below, and double heighted spaces. An infill of structural acrylic allows some of these apertures to be occupied not only through vision, but by foot. Other aperture moments can also be occupied or sat upon, through an infill of hammock netting.

Inspired by, and referential to, the landscape of Newfoundland, moments of intimacy and expansive vault-like spaces provide an array of programmatic possibilities.

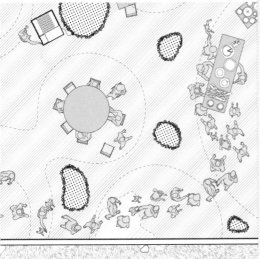

DIRT AND ROCKS AND MAYBE LOGS AND THINGS
Paul Preissner

Xuexia Li

The notion of Anti-Gravity has been inherited in the subconscious of human beings since the myth of the Sisyphus. Through the research of the natural material "boulder," I would like to embody this perceptual feeling through architectural expression. The two materials used are the heavy concrete blocks that were "found" with artificial cut edge, while preserving the natural breakage; and the granite "boulders" with various shapes and sizes. The boulders are framed into rectangular shapes through transparent resin and used as main structural supports for lifting the heavy blocks, while imbedded boulders can also be treated as individual exhibitions that are floating around the entire building.

On the ground floor, an open plaza is designed as a microcosm with the landscape elements of St John's: the stairs of the amphitheater echo the slanted fossil rocks of Mistaken Point, and the meander paths around a central pond that are experienced in Signal Hill.

For the massing composition, the Heavy blocks are raised up to different heights and connected through stairs. Placing the more public programs on the top floor encourages people to wander around the building and be bewildered by the organization of spaces.

The entire project aims at arousing a feeling of a delicate balance between the calmed Zen of the boulders and the seemingly fragility of structure.

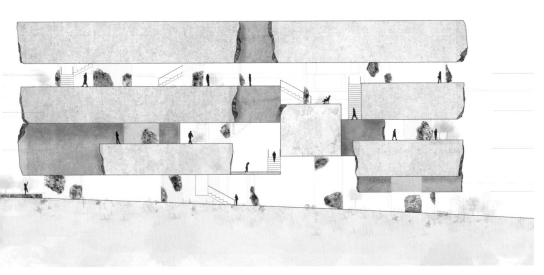

MULTIFARIOUS MATTER:
LES HALLES 2030
Robert Stuart-Smith
Musab Badahdah (TA)

Assistant Professor of
Architecture, Stuart Weitzma
School of Design, Principal
Research Associate, Universi
College of London: Computer
Science, Director of The
Autonomous Manufacturing L
(Penn & UCL), Director
of Robert Stuart-Smith Desig
& Kokkugia, M.Arch & Urbanis
Architectural Association
School of Architecture, Londe

Cemex collaborators:
    Davide Zampini
    Carlos Enrique Terrado
    Alexandre Guerin

Urban retail is undergoing a significant transformation due to the rise of online shopping. Amazon Go is the first supermarket to allow customers to walk out without paying at a register, while a suite of new fashion boutiques utilize virtual assistants to deliver clothing to changing rooms at the touch of a button. Beyond novelty, these applications of technology transform not only the experience of shopping, but also the square footage, fit-out, staffing, security, supply and delivery logistics. Apple's park-bench and tree-scape interiors, or Nike's half-court basketball facilities have become a destination in themselves. Extending beyond merchandise, experience is ultimately part of their product, producing a fuzzy edge to public space, capable of enhancing our urban experiences.

Inspired by Levi Bryant's Democracy of Objects and Stan Allen's Field Conditions, the studio operated through both object and field, embracing all site objects and actors as active participants in design expression and considering them as integral to architecture. Material considerations were also investigated through the designing of effects strategized through fabrication methods developed within a collaborative workshop at Cemex's Global Research Centre in Switzerland during Travel Week.

Reacting to Uber's recent €25 Million investment into Paris Air-Taxi research, the studio explored a speculative near-present future, a post-human retail and public space in the context of emerging autonomous transportation infrastructure including e-scooters, air-taxis, autonomous cars and delivery bots in one of central Paris's most important transportation and retail hubs; Les Halles. Les Halles functioned as a market until a central and suburban railway station and shopping centre was constructed in 1971. The development was ambitious yet is considered a socio-political failure, entrapping suburbanites within its interior rather than facilitating their integration with the city, and became appropriated by fast-food venues and drug addicts. Its inadequacies were addressed by the recent construction of a new retail centre. Berger Anziutti Architects's "La Canopée" enlarged the park, physically connecting it to a pedestrian concourse that crosses central Paris through to the Pompidou Centre in Beaubourg. While La Canopée is an improvement, it did not challenge our existing concept of retail. An opportunity remains in re-considering the nature of urban park and retail as a Posthuman entrepreneurial proposition, which may involve a downsizing, up-sizing or a redistribution of space for shoppers versus goods and entertainment or wellness vs retail. While Paris has been the site of seminal urban park concepts, Bernard Tschumi and OMA's competition proposals for Park de la Villette are now 35 years old. The rise of Industry 4.0 may be potentially destabilizing to urban space as is currently known, yet it offers new opportunities for establishing complex and dynamic relationships between a park's myriad of occupants, from human gatherings to autonomous garbage disposal vehicles. The studio explored alternative concepts for re-casting public space adjacent to new models of retail in this socio-political and economically charged Parisian transportation hub.

Partner: Cemex Global Research HQ, Switzerland
Location: Biel and Basel, Switzerland, and Paris, France

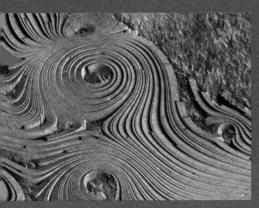

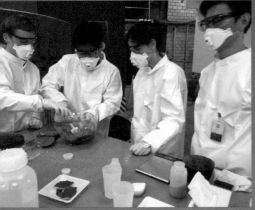

MULTIFARIOUS MATTER: LES HALLES 2030
Robert Stuart-Smith

Qiaoxi Liu, Yuwei Wang

With an increase in online retail we position the Les Halles site in Paris as a hub for health and wellness programs and shopping that provides a similar, if not higher level of privacy than online stores. Upon arrival by air-taxi or autonomous car, a visitor receives an AI-trained health and wellness evaluation and can then make use of this data for various meditation, fitness, or shopping activities that take place within one space, with advanced robot systems delivering clothing and other goods to shoppers rather than requiring shoppers to circulate publicly through stores. The design integrates the transport vehicles within the architectural language of the project, and distributes them adjacent to park canyons and waterfalls occupied by people and retail fulfillment and storage connected to the vehicles by product transportation tubes. The design is situated quite low on the Les Halles site, infilling the already existing deep basement with program, while keeping surrounding neighborhood visible.

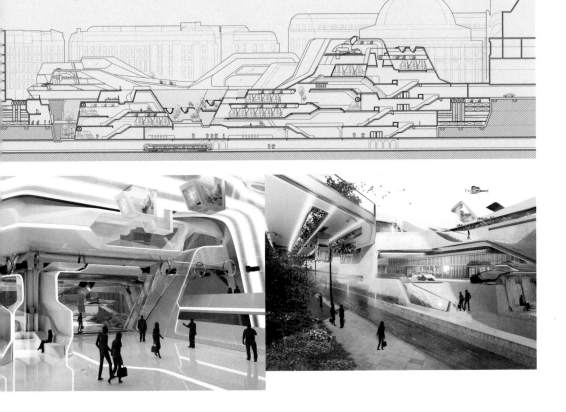

MULTIFARIOUS MATTER:
LES HALLES 2030
Robert Stuart-Smith

Khondaker Rahman, Hasan Uretmen

The Les Halles site in Paris is a hub for retail and transport. With the increase in online shopping, the site is converted to a fulfillment center, which utilizes air-taxis and drones to deliver packages to the surrounding quarters of the city. This shift to online shopping makes aisle browsing and window shopping redundant, replaced by a suite of augmented-reality (AR) viewing rooms that can be booked out for periods of time where visitors can be immersed in the products and environments they may wish to purchase. An AR fashion parade is also coupled with a bar, where each visitor is witnessing a customized and different version of the show. These spaces leverage a hybrid of physical and virtual space, as does the exterior public spaces where Pokemon's, virtual chess and other activities enable the spaces to be reprogrammed throughout each day to suit different visitor's interests. A viewing area called the "hive" in the center of the site enables visitors to witness the bustle of many drones coming and going delivering goods from the center.

SEPTEMBER 26TH, 2018
MEMORY/RACE/NATION:
THE POLITICS OF MODERN MEMORIALS
Mabel O. Wilson

The Memorial to Enslaved Laborers at the University of Virginia's (UVA) grounds

The project was designed in a collaboration between Howeler + Yoon Architecture, Dr. Mabel O. Wilson (Studio&), Gregg Bleam Landscape Architect, and Dr. Frank Dukes. Together, the design team led an extensive community engagement and design process. Images: Courtesy Howeler + Yoon Architecture LLP

OCTOBER 29TH, 2018
COMPOUND BEINGS, OTHER NATURES
Simon Kim

Tesla House, Ibañez Kim

Polyhouse, Ibañez Kim

NOVEMBER 7TH, 2018
BEYOND SURFACE
Dorit Aviv

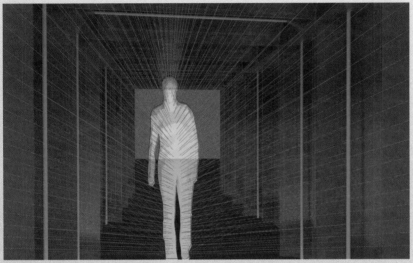

Diagram of radiant temperature exchange between the human body and its surrounding in the thermal installation space at the Seoul Biennale for Architecture and Urbanism

ADVANCED'
by Ferda Kolatan, Coordinator

The Architecture 704 Design Research Studio is an in-depth exploration of various architectural topics through rigorous conceptual thinking and advanced design methodologies. The primary goal of this final design studio of the Master of Architecture program is to equip the outgoing students with the ability to formulate a research interest, which reaches beyond graduation and puts them on a path to becoming leaders in the field of architecture.

The challenges for architects today are unprecedented as multiple trajectories define the territories in which we operate. From global economic markets shaping our cities to the ecological realities of the Anthropocenic age, we find ourselves entangled in forces, which are seemingly elusive and yet impact our profession profoundly. In addition, new media and technology have given us powerful tools for design, which we are still in the process of understanding and developing. While individual technologies have matured enough to generate new formalisms, larger questions pertaining subsequent cultural effects are subject to current, and often contentious, debate. If one of architecture's main characteristics is to materially express the contemporary context within which it operates, then we are finding ourselves in the exciting position to provide a vision for a new paradigm. This paradigm cannot be simply rooted in prior models of thought and design but must progressively and unwaveringly engage in the now.

The Design Research Studio takes on this challenge and explores—through the individual expertise of leading architects in the field—various strategies and speculations that actively shape our environment, present and future. In this context we view design-research as both the indispensable element through which we critically reflect on our world as well as the laboratory in which specific and sophisticated design solutions are tested and applied.

NEXT GENERATION AIRPORT TERMINALS
Masoud Akbarzadeh
Mostafa Akbari (TA)

Director of the Polyhedral Structures Laboratory. PhD the Institute of Technology in Architecture, ETH Zurich, in Architecture Studios (Computation) and M.Arch from MIT

In the most recent assessment examining current infrastructure conditions of the US, needs, capacity, and safety, American Society of Civil Engineers (ASCE) graded the overall quality of the US infrastructures as D+, rated from A to D where A is exceptional and fit for future and D is poor and at risk. Most of the infrastructural projects in the US were built in the '50s and '60s and were aimed to serve almost 50 years. Those projects need to be replaced immediately including half of the existing bridges in the country (*The Economist*, June 17th, 2014).

The ASCE grade for the aviation infrastructure is D. Although aviation industry uses technologically advanced aircrafts, their receiving airport infrastructures heavily suffer from the lack of the equivalent facilities and organization systems to handle large passenger traffics. The most recent major airport in the US was built almost 20 years ago in Denver and stays in the 28th place in the annual ranking of the top 100 airports in the world together with Boston Logan airport in 89th place according to Skytrax. Crumbling infrastructures will limit the US ability to contribute to the ever-growing global economy of the future. Thus, reconstructing/replacing the deteriorating infrastructures is unavoidable.

Indeed, architects should play a significant role in designing and rethinking the future of infrastructures. In response, this studio aims to research the formal and organizational configuration of the next generation of infrastructures specifically airports.

The architecture of the future will be positively affected by technology: the technological advances in the transportation industries such as drone taxis and Hyperloop will change our perception of commuting, transitional space, and the so-called terminals. The terminals will be where the interstitial spaces occur at the intersection of multiple transportation modes, and therefore pose an interesting architectural question for us: what is the terminal of the future?

Designing such architectural spaces requires utilizing specific structures. In fact, the studio will concentrate on the development of non-conventional architectural structures that can respond to the needs of such spaces and programs more succinct than the conventional solutions.

Therefore, the main research objectives of the studio can be summarized as follows:
- formal structural explorations of the efficient structural typologies suitable for infrastructural design;
- material computing research including tectonic studies on the design of structural forms using various construction materials and prefabrication techniques including wood, stone, brick, concrete, steel, carbon fiber, etc;
- programmatic studies of the future airport terminals including the integration of high-speed ground transportation station with drone port;
- and finally the architectural design of the space to manifest the research.

NEXT GENERATION AIRPORT TERMINALS
Masoud Akbarzadeh

Qi Liu, Zehua Qi

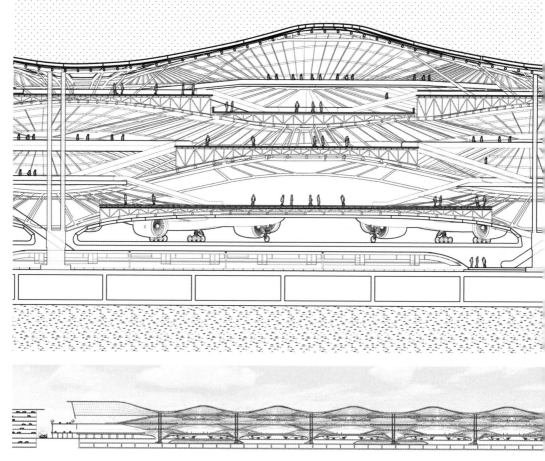

The Project Interweave is a reimagination of the Philadelphia International Airport. The project started with exploration of structural and form possibilities which are appropriate for a future airport design. Through various studies and tests we produced a structure and form system attractive in its form and efficient for the airport program. Through our analysis the future airport is going to be more diverse, more condensed and more focused on multiple layers of transportations. Our airport has four levels which are inter-connected with very gentle slopes with moving belt to provide visitors more smooth and pleasant experience moving between different levels. The unground level is the high-speed train running parallel with the building so travelers can get access to the get from any section of the building via public transportation. The second level is the arrival level which is directly connect to the public highway and easy access to the high-speed train underground. The third level will serve as the departure level which will incorporate various programs like shopping, catering, exhibition and performing. The top level is designed to be a public zone with abundant natural light and public space. Overall, the project is intended to bring up a new type of traveling experience that visitors can transit between different programs smoothly and seamlessly.

NEXT GENERATION AIRPORT TERMINALS
Masoud Akbarzadeh

Yuchen Liu, Ye Huang

The new "Floating Cloud" terminal uses the contrast of lightness and heaviness to express the elegance of structure and the continuous surface flow of internal space. From the outside, the internal space resembles a cloud floating above the ground. We started the design with force and form finding methods to generate a structure system that could not only respond to different types of future flying machines, but also respond to human needs. The branching structural system accommodates all the pogrom spaces and gate systems to increase the efficiency and spatial quality of the overall airport.

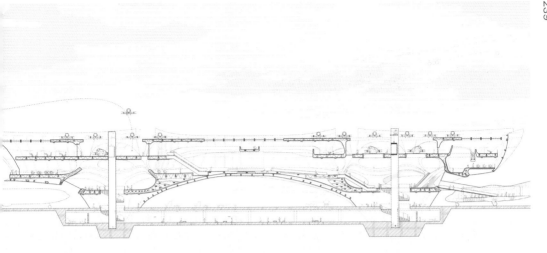

COLOMBO INTERNATIONAL FINANCIAL CITY - SRI LANKA
Cecil Balmond, Ezio Blasetti
Drew Busmire (TA)

CRITIC: CECIL BALMOND, EZIO BLASETTI

Cecil Balmond: Founder of Balmond Studio, Chairman of Arup's European Building Division, Ran the AGU (Advan Geometry Unit) design group, B.Sc. from University of Southampton, M.Sc. from Imperial College of Scie London, D.Sc. from University of Southampton

Ezio Blasetti: Co-Founder of Ahylo, M.S. in Advanced Architectural Design from Columbia University

This research studio investigated non-linear algorithmic procedures at both a methodological and tectonic level. This exploration took the form of design research, which was tested through a rigorous urban and architectural proposal.

The studio generated a multidimensional terrain of data, which attempted to capture and compress the various infrastructural, environmental, and architectural parameters of the site. This abstract construction was our conceptual and literal site of intervention. Design operated as a feedback tool of navigation and adaptation. The studio reexamined and critiqued the developer's masterplan and proposed an alternative future for the site. The participants in the studio collaborated to provide a unique and inspired urban vision and gradually focused on six pivotal projects at the building scale. Working in feedback between the various scales, from the regional to the tectonic, allowed the studio to speculate on the limits of architecture as an organizational, structural and aesthetic agent.

Central to the studio agenda is the exploration of algorithmic systems and their application to design. This involves extracting the processes that operate within the physical world as well as developing new models of organization. Students are encouraged to engage closely with computational processes and to develop protocols of data mining and interaction. The studio functions as an open source research group of computational design. It combines the larger resource of algorithmic and parametric modules developed for a series of programming languages.

Our studio approaches computation as a new fundamental logos at once analytical and generative. Our speculative condition is that computation is not solely digital but omnipresent. We approach computation as a generative framework for urban morphology and as an embodied infrastructure within the city itself. As such, beyond the correlation of simulation, this studio positions different mediums onto a flat ontology and mines the collateral effects of the synchronicities and divergences between them. Digitization is thus the key to what Manuel De Landa calls a flat ontology, "one made exclusively of unique, singular individuals, differing in spatio-temporal scale, but not in ontological status."

Charles Sanders Peirce, a philosopher of logic, broke down hypothesis into induction and abduction. In simple words, for Pierce; Deduction looks at the past, Induction generalizes for a particular present and Abduction (or what is commonly called speculation) points at the future, or "possible futures." The idea is that abduction has the potential of suggesting something new. Similar to Steven Shaviro's "Discognition," we asked what does it mean to be "Thinking Like a City?"

Studio Collaborators: Balmond Studio, CHEC Port City Colombo
Location: Colombo, Sri Lanka

COLOMBO INTERNATIONAL FINANCIAL CITY - SRI LANKA
Cecil Balmond, Ezio Blasetti

Yifei Chen, Thomas Yun

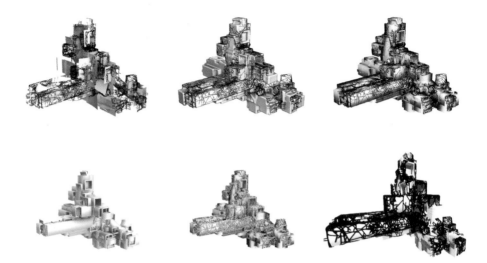

Infrapolis is a project that speculates on a future where the city develops from a network of infrastructures created through a recursive branching system. Infrastructure in this case can be many things, whether it is transportation infrastructure in the form of roads, railways, and pedestrian, utilities such as water, sewage, gas or electric, or even social infrastructure such as schools, hospitals, and emergency personnel. The concept is derived from a speculation of a future where algorithmic systems can develop and regulate infrastructural needs in order to meet the demands of an ever growing urban fabric. The systems generated from our project hopes to create a city that is interconnected and reorganize the complex networks of the urban fabric.

When projecting into the future, the project seeks to rethink the concept of roads and the tendency of cities to be organized around them. Roads are a critical aspect of how modern society navigates and identifies themselves within a city. The aspect of location becomes defined by the positioning of the road, as the idea of addresses and directioning naturally follow the naming conventions of roads. However, with future developments in real time location tracking and positional data, as well as the expansion of autonomous vehicles and delivery systems, we speculate that the city becomes no longer bound to a set of roads as its main method of spatial organization. Thus the lines generated from our systems can embody much more complex systems of organization.

In the building scale the branching algorithm creates space in 3 structures. The primary system, which creates the initial building volume is composed of what we defined as spatial infrastructure, which includes corridors, vertical circulation, and accessible pathways. Within the boundaries of this primary volume, we generate a secondary system, which we assign as utility infrastructure, in the form of plumbing, HVAC systems, electric and data lines. These systems typically inhabit the interiors of walls and floors of buildings, thus the lines are extended as planes that create the walls and floors of our building, creating interior space. The final tertiary system is then generated along the surfaces created by the primary and secondary systems, providing the tectonic and architectural detailing that create our design.

COLOMBO INTERNATIONAL FINANCIAL CITY - SRI LANKA

Cecil Balmond, Ezio Blasetti

Yihao Zhang, Andi Zhang

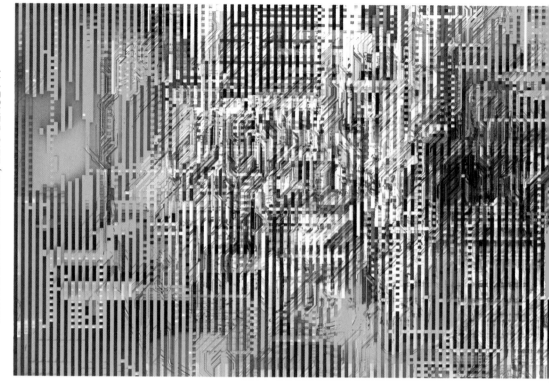

One of the main goals of our project was to challenge the traditional notion of the ground in terms of its arrangement on the site in Colombo, Sri Lanka. During our trip, our attention was drawn to the hot and humid climate and the heavy traffic in the city of Colombo. Our design intends to increase the connectivity of the site and the continuity of the urban fabric. Covered and Semi-open public spaces of urban flow and leisure work as a network, connecting indoor spaces and creating a well tempered continuity between interior and exterior.

Our project is a terraforming negotiation between different elements. Instead of designing an independent building, we are trying to mix the components between the ground, water, air, and buildings by drifting the components around in a algorithmic ways, generating a splitting, merging, and blurring effect. Water will flow into the buildings and buildings will submerge into the ground. The various combinations of different elements allow for the mix of programs in an extended zone of civic space, where the boundaries between architecture and the environment are blurred.

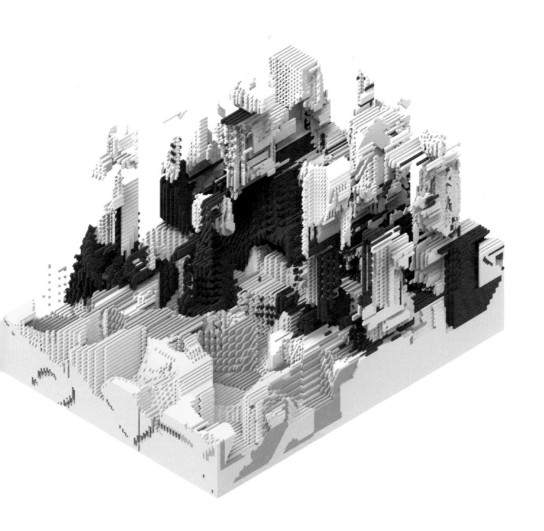

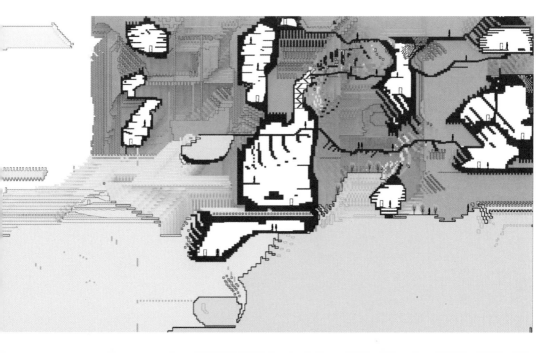

CALAMITY LIBRARY
Winka Dubbeldam
Matthijs Bouw (Guest Critic and Resilience Consultant)
Ryan Barnette (TA)

Winka Dubbeldam: Miller Professor and Chair of Architecture, Founder and Principal of Archi-Tectonics, M.Arch from the Institute of Higher Professional Architect Education, Rotterdam (1990), MS-AAD from Columbia (1992

Matthijs Bouw: Associate Professor Practice, Rockefelle Urban Resilience Fellow, McHa Center Fellow for Risk and Resilience, Founder of One Architecture

Political dynamics, climate change, and demographic changes are contemporary global challenges. In our research-based teaching, we rely on a holistic methodology and an inter-culturally engaged design network to bring about future-oriented architectural answers to worldwide issues.

The 2019 collaborative workshop will specifically focus on global ecological challenges concerning architecture and water. Themes like climate change, politics, and infrastructure, will form the lenses to understand contemporary cities in the context of a transforming environment. Flooding, drought and other forms of extreme weather are observed more and more as normal occurrences everywhere on the planet. The impact of urbanization, its global reaches into rural, oceanic, and atmospheric environments, has become immense. Human impact thus forms an ongoing feedback loop of dynamic interactions between the built and non-built environment.

The river environments of the Spree and the Mississipi are two focus areas identified for the projects of the workshop. The long-term interactions between humans and water along rivers will be analyzed and discussed as catchment areas for ecological, technological, industrial and social realities. Topics of spatio-temporal transformations like mobility, pollution, and resource extraction will be looked at as water culture that is both human and non-human in order to inform future oriented design projects.

Thus, the workshop will engage with these topics in active design research. Students will prepare presentations before their arrival on the context and thematic content of their project interest. During the workshop week, design projects will be brainstormed and developed in groups and partner work.

The main teaching goal of the workshop is to support student projects dealing with complex global themes, done in an intensive week-long collaborative workshop environment. The architectural projects should reach a level of rigorous complexity with thorough programming. The students are thus challenged to grasp the design question and its implications in order to clarify it analytically. Then, they formulate a conceptual idea as a solution. The experimental and methodological processes develops into an architectural design with a subject-specific focus. Students engage in finding architectural solutions through the design process and in clearly communicating and discussing their ideas. Throughout, the students will be consistently accompanied in their projects by individual and group tutorials with assistant professors as well as presentations with the lead professors.

Additional informative input will come from invited lectures and excursions into Berlin's history and interaction between water and architecture, for example, including visits to municipal brick water towers, the Ludwig Leo Bau (Versuchsanstalt für Wasserbau und Schiffbau), the Ökohaus by Frei Otto, the proposed Flussbad site, as well as a city history tour about the Spree and Berlin's canals. Students will also participate in the ongoing Anthropocene Curriculum at the Haus der Kultur der Welt, which currently has a research project on the Mississippi River. The workshop will end with formal presentations with an invited jury and a reflective discussion about the experimental work done during the week.

Studio Funding: DAAD via TU Braunschweig
Location: Berlin, Germany

THE STATE OF WATER // THE ANTHROPOCENE
Matthijs Bouw, Winka Dubbeldam

CRITIC: WINKA DUBBELDAM, MATTHIJS BOUW

Alexandra Adamski, Logan Weaver

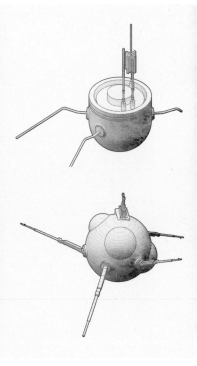

New Normals aims to create a series of resilient architectures that can be deployed to areas of the Mississippi whose current built environments are insufficient to withstand the natural events of the Anthropocene. Flooding, storms, climate change, and erratic weather patterns push back against the current state of the river and threaten to cause expensive and irreversible damage to contemporary human interventions. In the near future, events that are currently considered catastrophic will become commonplace, and human habitation will prove unsustainable. Our project begins with the idea that architecture can play a role in creating sustainable and resilient ways to live in a world where calamities are normalized.

New Normals embraces the Anthropocene and its climatic conditions as a challenge and opportunity to create innovative and lasting designs. Its brand suggests that human culture has the ability to survive in the Anthropocene, but must embrace a way of living that is, as yet, unfamiliar. To this extent, New Normals helps to usher in this new way of life in a gradual but assertive manner, preparing humanity for a new set of ecological and cultural imperatives.

The initial project is proposed as a government-funded venture through which the Upper St. Anthony Lock and Dam (which in its decommissioned state is costing the government over $3 million a year in maintenance fees) can be repurposed and reactivated as an economically-productive entity. The satellites that are produced on site are commissioned by communities in areas that are in danger. This requires potentially connecting to local economies and governments that wish to outpace imminent calamities and avoid the expensive damages that will inevitable be caused by increased floods and other natural disasters. The project's profitability relies on the ability of the initial investors to embrace the long-term benefits of manufacturing and installing resilient architectures.

THE STATE OF WATER // THE ANTHROPOCENE
Matthijs Bouw, Winka Dubbeldam

CRITIC: WINKA DUBBELDAM, MATTHIJS BOUW

Xinyi Chen, Zhenqin Dong

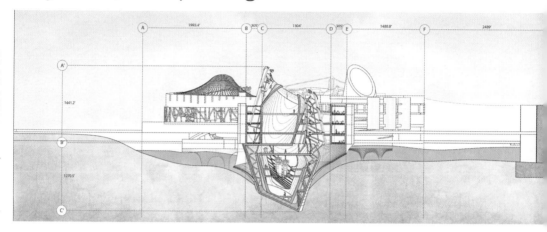

The "Ongoing Green" is an energy production project, hybridized on the existing lock 26 in the city of Alton along Mississippi river. Envisioning a new energy economic cycle, this new assemblage localizes power generation, boosts local economy, and greatly alleviates manmade damages to the Mississippi river through the adoption and planning of clean algae industry and its related byproducts.

The project features an algae energy production plant, providing the Alton city and the other cities along Mississippi river with clean electricity power as well as resources for future development and research. The byproducts of algae, including the biofuel used for transportation and food for consumption, also facilitates the completion of a brand-new eco-friendly production loop. The associate waterfront park mitigates the intensity of flooding caused by traditional levees and provides the algae farms with intermittent nutrition and protection.

The proposal is for a 20-acre, 20-MW Green Energy Production and Innovation Hub located on the Mississippi River near the city of Alton (integrating the original Lock #26), and together with an urban masterplan, redeveloping old industrial areas along the river bank linked to the proposed Hub and bounded by Highway 67, Highway 3 and East Broadway.

As a milestone project proposed for the city of Alton, the 20-MW Algae Biomass Energy Production Hub together with the urban strategy steps away from the traditional large-scale (500MW) energy production from coal burning, localizing small-scale green energy production, largely reducing pollution and inefficient transportation of resources. The development and future operation of the project creates job opportunities and brings in green-technology talents to the city of Alton, exacerbating the economic growth. The proposed water-landscape, softens the edges between the city and the river, increases water infiltration, and mitigates potential flooding. The projected public education center and the water park are free for public, bringing residents from inland to the water, promoting green energy education in a fun way while raising public awareness for environmental protection. By organizing social events and activities at the education center and water park, a strong social community is fostered, information flow is encouraged, and inputs from the local residents are collected for future improvement. Finally, the embracement of green industry and the notion of "going green" creates a new identity for the city of Alton, which will make its influence to the surrounding cities.

HOUSE OF TOMORROW
Homa Farjadi
Chang Yuan Max Hsu (TA)
Anna Ishii (TA)

M.Arch, RIBA, ARB, Principal of Farjadi architects in Lond Professsor in Practice of Architecture at the Universi of Pennsylvania, responsible for the teaching of the Lond Studio at the Architectural Association, London, unit ma at the AA School of Architectu 1980-88, associate professor arch GSD Harvard Universit 1989-96 and has held chaire visiting professorships at Ya UPenn and Edinburgh univer ties, as well as visiting profes ships at Columbia university and University of Virginia in the US, and Karlsruhe Univer in Germany

The studio topic is a speculation on the house of the future. Both in its singular form and as variations of multiples have in many ways been central for architecture and urbanism. In framing styles of living, in constructing versions of community and gradations of public and private domains, in their intersection with other geographic and programmatic formulation of work, leisure, and life, design of housing can be said to have historically set up primary criteria for scaling spaces of domestic life as well as structural formation of cities. In our project the design of the contemporary house will be driven by two sets of speculative frames.

Iñaki Ábalos' *The Good Life* visits seven houses of modernity to describe how ideas and ways of thinking about the good life in each intersects with formation of space of the house, planning and living in it not as manuals for forms of domestic architecture but a map of the crossing of the two modes of thinking. The second text in design form is proposed by Alison and Peter Smithson in 1956 as the House of the future for the Daily Mail Ideal Home exhibi-tion. It is a pleasurable example of speculation on the effect of new technologies and new cultural mores for the design of the house of the future.

Both texts are taken up in the methods of analysis they offer in designing and reading of space of the house, of the sites they construct, the technolo-gies they employ, objects and furniture they import and where elements of the architecture come to touch our lives and ways we live within and around it. Houses here construct ideas as much as they are constructed by them through contemporary positions of their protagonists. Our studio project will use the two texts as interlocutors speculating on the contemporary parameters and potentials of the house designed for tomorrow now.

In considering the two texts in the US context, the project for the house of the future will consider processual thinking focused by Land Art move-ment as a radical reframing of private visions of manmade interventions in nature. These will offer set of parameters for its siting between the artificial and the natural landscape of the urban and the open country. The house and the site will be an occasion to speculate on attitudes towards new technolo-gies, environmental processes, work/art and habits and economies of daily life as they will affect space making around versions of domestic life where Art and life find overlapped boundaries and work on the landscape constructs new encounters between abstract vision and embodied experience.

The studio trip to Marfa Texas, the Chianti foundation, will engage with the siting of work/ life of Donald Judd which offers a radical reoccupation of site of work and daily life of the artist.

Location: Marfa, TX

HOUSE OF TOMORROW
Homa Farjadi

Yanan Bella Ding

In contemporary society, the concept of "family" is becoming less and less important to some people. For these people, they yearn for freedom, joy, and are unwilling to be bound by inherent systems of the city and stay stable at one living space. They become the nomadic tribes of society. Different from the traditional fixed residential form led by traditional family perspective, nomadic houses rely more on changeable natural conditions and resources, such as light and shade, rain and wind in different moments. Thus, a house with mobility and dynamics will be more suitable for nomads to live and offer diverse possibilities for nomads to choose. Combing with concepts mentioned in *The Good life*, the project is aiming at constructing a nomadic living system, an operative system, to provide a set of houses for the future.

HOUSE OF TOMORROW
Homa Farjadi

Yefan Zhang

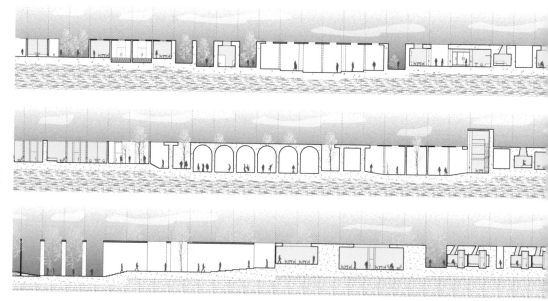

Co-Living-Working "Field" is the key concept of the project, but mainly focusing on spatial quality and materiality itself, not only limited in the functionalism. The preliminary research mainly focused on Andy Warhol's the factory as modern loft space and minimalist artist Carl Andre's sculptures and poems scripts. Warhol's studio is described as an urban commune, a "party" space for work, artistic creation and other activities, which is disordered, unpredictable and improvised with minimum privacy. However, the art pieces of Carl Andre's poems are always ordered in linear and grid format with seriality.

The concept of the design based on the "Field" or co-living, co-working and other daily activities in an abstract flow of chance, which focuses on space organized in specific order looking for effect of seriality as a reduction of authorial composition so it would be sharing side by side rather. The relationship between publicity and privacy, interior and exterior, inflexibility and fixation, unpredictability and certainty, permanent and temporary in architectural language of the design becomes finding their chance spatiality within this abstract geometry prompt initial organizational ideas. The landscape of Marfa, Texas is considered as the site offering a typical American landscape of sparsely occupied land to offer a speculation on future of the house, where domestic space intersects with free flow of chance daily work and pleasure in the matrix of 'the Warholian party' on the Field.

The "Field" in this project is based on a 1000x1000 Feet site in Marfa, containing all of the daily living and working system for the residents. For Co-Living in the future, the definition of living will not be divided into living room, dining or kitchen space anymore. Residents only have their own individual sleeping cells and private toilets. The other living space all become flexible and sharing place without specific functional limitation. Additionally, the future Co-Working space will also not be restricted into typical shared workspaces or office layouts, but free work, communication or meeting could happen anywhere.

15 MINUTES AND COUNTING
Hina Jamelle
Caleb White (TA)

Architect and Director, Contemporary Architecture Practice, New York (2002) and Shanghai (2014), Awarded Fifty Under Fifty: Innovators of the 21st Century (2015), Awarded Architectural Record Design Vanguard Award (2004), Author: *Elegance. Architectu Design*, John Wiley and Sons Inc London. (2007)

"The idea is not to live forever; it is to create something that will."
-Andy Warhol

Pop Art in the West emerged in the post-war period as an ironic, self-examining, but enthusiastic look at the mass imagery of our consumerist society. Pop Art stood firmly at the cross roads of the elite avant-garde of the art world and the broader interests of popular culture and society at large.

The Andy Warhol Foundation is the global keeper of Andy Warhol's legacy. One of the foundation's goals is to increase its influence and visibility and a new museum in the international gateway city of Miami, Florida is a strategic one. The Miami Design District is an 18-square block creative neighborhood dedicated to innovative fashion, design, art, architecture. After decades of falling urban decay, the Design District has risen to fame as a destination for the arts and design.

The goal for each student is to evaluate the potentials of artistic techniques in designing architecture that flows from topological surfaces and spatial arrangements, and to apply these to a range of familiar architectural issues. The final proposal of each student will emerge out of an inter-related working method between artistic techniques, program, space, atmosphere, and materials that combine to develop an innovative new museum formation.

Location: Miami, FL

15 MINUTES AND COUNTING
Hina Jamelle

John Dunn, Yiran Fu

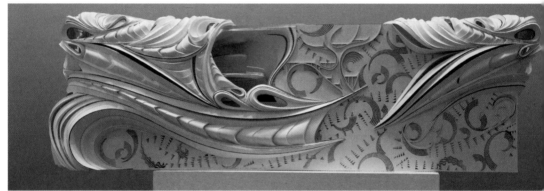

Our new Warhol Museum in Miami speculates on the architectural possibilities of pop art techniques popularized by Andy Warhol. Our design research focused specifically on the concepts of the Superflat: Color, Visual Paths, Speeds, Scale and Rotation are studied and translated into architectural form and space.

The Superflat is a pop art methodology and philosophy established by Takashi Murakami. Two principles of the Superflat were of particular interest to us: 1. The control of the viewers eye across art works and 2. Scalar Shifts and Rotations from profile to elevation. Our project pursues ways these principles can apply to Architecture.

At the site in the Design District—the Museum's north and east exterior elevations are designed to transition from one to the other effortlessly. Large concrete volumes highlighted with embedded copper seams allow for a smooth continuous visual path across the exterior that pulls your eye across its soft corners-culminating in the museum's entrance. Scaler shifts occur on two levels—between the larger and smaller galleries and the transition between smooth and intricate materials. Public circulation in the larger galleries is at a faster pace allowing one to take in larger amounts of artworks while the smaller galleries are designed and materially detailed for longer and more intimate experiences with the art works on view. Transition between these spaces is gradual and fluid, resulting in a interior organization that guides visitors through multiple fluid sequences of spatial experiences. The interplay between larger concrete volumes and smaller scaled intricate metal panels emphasize this experience via natural and artificial light.

The use of the Superflat and the development of architectural techniques related to it, have allowed us to establish a new unique museum organization and aesthetic for a Pop Art Museum.

15 MINUTES AND COUNTING
Hina Jamelle

Lingyun Yang, Yingxin Zhang

Pop Art has a plethora of techniques to stimulate architectural design research. Inspired by Pop Artists' painting techniques, we focused on interlocking, nesting and repetition techniques. On the Museum's Façade, techniques of interlocking and nesting were developed into varying solids and voids with varying scales and depth. Within the museum the interlocking technique allows us to develop a nested relationship between interior and exterior spaces via a series of external courtyards connected to galleries. Repetitions of nesting techniques achieve the continuity of space and create an atmosphere of Pop Art spirit.

Color has an important role in pop art paintings and in our museum sited in Miami's Design District. We set up a series of principles of color in our museum. By using color in different location in the surface or the aperture, color can indicate different function of inner spaces. We also paint the courtyard from wall to floor using one color to distinguish the external and internal space. Those principles also help us codify the façade and achieve the "hyperpainterly" through the color of multiple adjacent surfaces in our Museum.

Together the techniques allow for visitors to experience a new kind of light filled and joyous museum experience for Miami.

ODDKIN ARCHITECTURE II // FOLLIES IN THE POSTINDUSTRIAL GARDEN
Ferda Kolatan
Michael Zimmerman (TA)

Ferda Kolatan, Assoc. Prof. of Practice, PennDesign, Founding Director of SU11 Architecture+Design, MsAAD Columbia University, Dipl.Ing. RWTH Aachen, Germany

CRITIC: FERDA KOLATAN

"Oddkin: Beings (and things) requiring each other in unexpected collaborations and combinations. Being situated someplace and not noplace, entangled and worldly."

> Donna Haraway, *Staying with the Trouble* (2016)

This 704 Design Research Studio examined new concepts for both the architectural folly and the garden in the postindustrial age. In architecture history the folly has occupied a curious niche as a seemingly non-essential or decorative element chiefly designed for pleasure and entertainment. As such it was commonly placed into landscapes and gardens heightening a sense of the picturesque and evoking idle fantasies without the burden of pragmatic use. Characteristically, the folly was a blend not only between garden and architecture but also of different stylistic forms and images, which were decontextualized and re-constructed in order to provoke new kinds of associations and imaginations.

In the late Baroque for instance the European "Lustgarten" would feature pavilions with motifs from far-away places (chinoiserie, arabesque, etc.). The goal was not simply to amuse the visitors but also to educate them about different cultures. Later, during the Romantic period, the English Garden deployed Greek temples and fake ruins to celebrate *sensibility* and counter the "cold," reason-driven world as typified by the industrial revolution. Here, the folly served as a critical tool to counter the alienation brought along by the early machine age and the rationalism with which it was associated.

Today, in our postindustrial and posthumanist age, the folly is due for a re-conceptualization. The chosen site in Istanbul is the old Ottoman Imperial Shipyard with obsolete machinery and functionalist architecture including three dry-docks for ship maintenance. The studio transformed the site into a contemporary folly garden by using the existing architecture and hybridizing it with new and foreign elements. In addition, 2D techniques of traditional Turkish water-painting (Ebru) were used to introduce colors and patterns to the projects.

As a guiding principle we were interested in Donna Haraway's notion of the *oddkin*. Haraway directs our attention toward odd couplings and hybrids as the real constituents of our contemporary world. By doing so, she challenges all predetermined cultural and ecological categories, which have privileged a ruthless anthropocentrism since the Enlightenment. The folly-garden with its deep history of classicist and romantic ideologies appears to be a perfect subject to be reinvented through the lens of the oddkin.

Studio Sponsor: GAD Foundation, Istanbul, Turkey

ODDKIN ARCHITECTURE II // FOLLIES IN THE POSTINDUSTRIAL GARDEN
Ferda Kolatan

Andrew Homick

Located within the Halic Imperial Shipyards in Karaköy, Istanbul, this project reimagines the basin as an archaeological curiosity; situated somewhere and no where, imposing a digital excavation of several fragmented architectural remains. As the follies in the Postindustrial garden are experienced via representation, they become fully autonomous objects. Embedded both positively and negatively, the remains become the outcome of a series of hybridized profile curves through which shadow projection is used to generate three-dimensional primitives.

ODDKIN ARCHITECTURE II // FOLLIES IN THE POSTINDUSTRIAL GARDEN
Ferda Kolatan

Xuexia Li

Paintscape is an idea for a post-industrial garden that turns the site of a historic imperial shipyard into a self-sustaining painting machine. As water collects within one of the shipyard's basins, it is pumped to a new level of the site in order to mix it with different colors of paint. The water is then released through different mechanisms to produce a variety of painterly effects that drip and run throughout the site. At times, the water washes down walls to produce large scale machine paintings, and in other instances, the water serves actual vegetation and water ponds to reshape the landscape and create unique garden experiences for visitors to enjoy. The pump and sprinkler systems are part of the garden experience, and they become part of the machine-like fountains and ornamental follies. A hydroelectric turbine is placed at the basin's main gate to capture the power of the water rushing in and re-use as electricity throughout the site. The Paintscape seeks to define a new aesthetic for a post-industrial garden by hybridizing parts of the existing basin infrastructure with pieces of nature, machine, and architecture into new, odd relationships.

FAKE NATURE
Florencia Pita
Caroline Morgan (TA)

Principal of FPmod, Co-Found of Pit & Bloom, Awarded a Fulbright-Fondo Nacional de l. Artes Scholarship to pursue studies at Columbia Universit (2000), MS-AAD from Columb Universtiy (2001), Graduated from National University of Rosario, Argentina, School of Architecture (1998)

CRITIC: FLORENCIA PITA

This studio will investigate the fabrication of artificial landscapes, within the context of industrial infrastructures and a river of concrete. The LA River is undergoing major transformation. What once was nature is now a hardscape of concrete that spans 51 miles. The potential of this river to shift from infrastructure to public spaces could transform the city of Los Angeles, and provide a new model of reuse, where active (as opposed to obsolete) infra- structure can perform multiple urban capacities. The LA River is not only an urban connector with an un-interrupted linear path, but also it carries water, which flows toward the ocean. This extravagant expenditure of water in a desert city seems paradoxical. This studio will take on the topic of FAKE NATURE. We will look at nature not for what it means but for what it exposes, a kind of semblance of nature.

The 'Los Angeles River Revitalization Master Plan' is an extensive proposal that takes into consideration the 51 miles of the LA river, our studio will focus on a particular area within the master plan which is located in Taylor Yard G2 River Park Project. The site is situated in the center of the LA Basin and in the middle of the Los Angeles River (at Mile 25) as it winds through Los Angeles County. The neighborhoods in this area are: Cypress Park, Glassell Park, Elysian Valley, Lincoln Heights, and Atwater Village. This span of the river is a "soft-bottomed" 11 mile stretch, therefore it houses a riparian ecosystem, in quite an opposing parallel to the rest of the river which is fully channelized.

The current proposal for the River Park Project at G2 presents a fully restored riparian landscape, a precious natural oasis in a context of concrete. This studio will look into novel ideas about nature. By challenging given con- ceptions in regard to what a park should be, we will research strategies to create FAKE NATURE. Roxy Paine's stainless steel tree is a reference on how a tree simulacrum (part tree, part plumbing, part machine) is a clear parallel to how we can articulate a tectonic forest by an artificial interpretation of nature. This class will "adapt" nature to architecture. We will look into "real" nature with Photogrammetry, and will convert the real to the artificial. The digital mesh will be scrutinized and represented into 3D-printed models. This feed- back process, from nature to artifice, will provide an array of geometries to design our parks and buildings.

Location: Los Angeles, CA

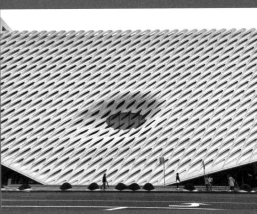

FAKE NATURE
Florencia Pita

Carla Bonilla, Joey Park

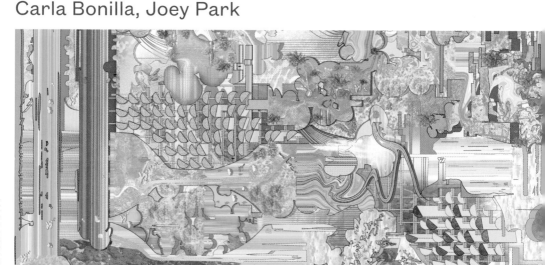

Plans to return the LA river to its "original wild" state fails to bring up the fact that the channel as it is now has its own kind of "wilderness." Patches of grass are growing in the rubble, and new forms of life are growing and developing within the concrete. This type of wilderness disregards boundaries between synthetic and natural, it generates fuzzy thresholds between one and the other. Having in mind this existing wilderness on the site, we explored how this ambiguous relationship between the synthetic and the natural could be further speculated on through drawing and pushed to generate a new synthetic wilderness, one that is truly representative of the existing "wild."

Fake Wild is a field in which elements merge and morph into one another. There are no clear thresholds between areas. There is not clear directionality. Actual wetlands are juxtaposed against synthetic distorted patterns of wetlands in an arbitrary and uncontrolled way, blurring their boundaries through their color and texture.

The natural and synthetic are juxtaposed in such a way in which there are both figures (paths and buildings) and fields (large patches of trees), as well elements in between. There are both soft and hard edges. Soft edges take the shape of river edges, creating fuzzy boundaries, and hard edges take the shape of circular and rectangular geometries. All of these conditions intermingle with one another all at once.

Carved out areas fill up according to water levels, which helps as a preventative measure against flooding. Under the platforms, water filtration machinery is placed. Water is transported to it through fields of pipes. These bundles of pipes run through the veins of the site, allowing for themselves to be seen and unseen at times. These fill up pools and lakes throughout the site. Within the most rigid part of the project, a grid holds viewing terraces and water tanks. These allow people to view this massive piece of land-art, allowing a tall and wide view of the fake wild.

Robert Smithson once said: "If art is about vision, can it also be about non vision...its form is a bi-polar notion that comes out of crystal structures... two separate things that relate to each other." Fake wild aims to explore an array of relationships that can be generated through the disruption of the synthetic-organic binary. A piece of land art that aims to express neither and both at the same time.

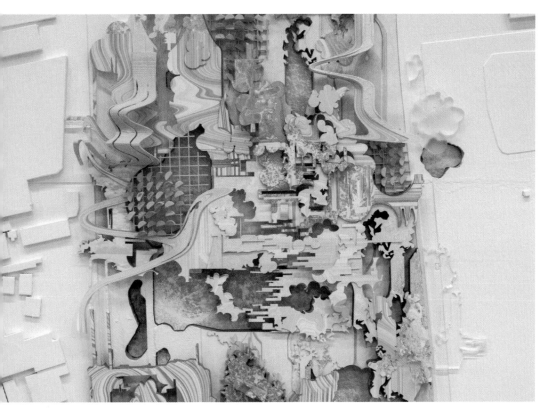

FAKE NATURE
Florencia Pita

Katie Lanski, Daniel Silverman

Gudea, ruler of Lagash in Neo-Sumeria once said: "He who controls the rivers controls life." This statement was certainly true 2000 years ago in southern Mesopotamia and continues to hold true today for the Los Angeles River. Mayor Eric Garcetti has described the river's current condition as being one that is confined by its "concrete straitjacket" and lack of civic vision. In order to remediate this, he is calling to install a string of public parks along its banks, declaring the G2 site the "crown jewel."

Our proposal for a park on the G2 site materializes as a tapestry of loomed gardens. The garden is inherently a space that negotiates the notion of the natural and the synthetic, the monumental and the domestic, the every day and the enchanted, and the permanent and the ephemeral; all attributes which are also descriptive of Los Angeles.

Jonathan Gold, LA's legendary food critic, spoke of Los Angeles as a city that has multiple cultures existing in parallel, but has few multicultural spaces/regions. Our collection of gardens becomes the principal node of multi-cultural exchange, catering to a diversity of ages, cultures, and beliefs.

The tapestry of loomed gardens manifests itself through an interplay between distinct fields and figures. The dispersed figures are unified together through the substrate-like field. The figures become the destination, while the field becomes the journey. The figures concentrate the multitudes through unique programmatic elements, producing a collection of public venues. Both destination and journey are of equal importance in the experience of the garden.

CONTEMPORARY DETAIL: CULTURAL CENTER FOR MIAMI'S DESIGN DISTRICT
Ali Rahim
Angela Huang (TA)

Architect and Director, Contemporary Architecture Practice, New York (2002) and Shanghai (2014), Awarded Fift' Under Fifty: Innovators of the 21st Century (2015), Awarded Architectural Record Design Vanguard Award (2004)

CRITIC: ALI RAHIM

Miami's Design District is the epicenter of design culture in Miami. It has become the hot spot for art galleries, boutique brands, and contemporary art museums. In designing a new cultural center for Miami's Design District we sought to push the envelope of contemporary design culture. Techniques are the hallmark of new technologies and put pressure on cultural development. The selection of a technique comes with a set of aesthetic values. We studied details in contemporary culture and shifted them into the discipline and the scale of architecture. Within the design process, it is common practice to work from a concept and increase the resolution in ever finer details and at a smaller scale. In this studio we reversed this process, designing the finest detail based on the possibilities of a manufacturing process accessible to the discipline of architecture. We will start with the detail of the surface and expand the detail to a volume and finally to the scale of experience.

Why the auto-industry? The automotive industry has traditionally been at the forefront of cutting-edge technologies, new manufacturing practices, and material sciences. The industry's leadership in these fields seems to be ever increasing. Over $100 billion dollars are spent on research and development annually. This far overshadows even the defense and aerospace industry's $22 billion annual spending on research. Over half of companies in the Dow Jones Industrial Average profit from the automobile industry. There are approximately 5000 auto industry patents filed globally each year which accounts for three to five percent of all patents—this is truly the vanguard of industrial and manufacturing research. The auto industry has also been leading the charge in terms of material innovation, developing next generation nanotechnology that can impact many industrial fields. Nano-tubes for fuel systems, ever lighter and more durable nano-composites, graphene which is 200 times stronger than steel and as thin as an atom) these are all examples of material innovations which could have massive impacts well beyond the auto industry. We researched, documented, and speculated on architecture using these innovations and paid particular attention to the detail.

Location: Miami, FL

CONTEMPORARY DETAIL: CULTURAL CENTER FOR MIAMI'S DESIGN DISTRICT
Ali Rahim

Mohamed Ali, Shih-Kai Lin

Adopting various methods of connection between the larger surface components of the shell and the contrasting finer details of the interior components was achieved through cradling, nesting, and revealing of certain elements. Spaces within the poche of the surfaces and the interiority of the components; as well as the residual between the two, define the occupiable experiences within the defined formal language. The bespoke details aim to embody a certain precision in the connection between the surfaces through delineated seams or reveals.

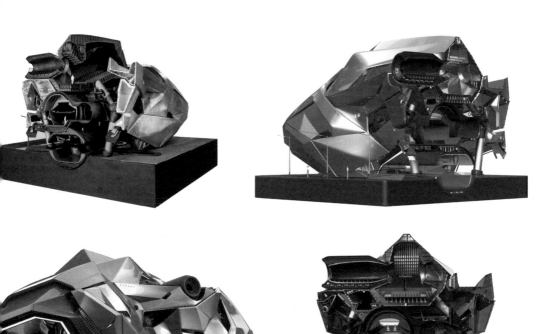

CONTEMPORARY DETAIL: CULTURAL CENTER FOR MIAMI'S DESIGN DISTRICT
Ali Rahim

CRITIC: ALI RAHIM

Luciano Najem, Ayotunde Ogunmoyero

This project looks at the relationship and dichotomy between the exteriority and interiority in which both sides are vastly different but at the same time, they help shape and support each other. The exterior of the building, like the exterior of the Bugatti Veyron, is characterized as being very smooth and BULBOUS. There is a fullness and volume to its form. The exterior is also LAYERED. There is an order and hierarchy to the monocoque carbon fiber exterior. Lastly, the exterior is heavily defined by the clean SEAMING. Most importantly, the center seaming that undergoes a couple of transformations as it makes its way around the building. All of this is made possible by the interior that is used to support the exterior. The more mechanical interior allows the exterior to be clean from structure and hardware as all of the "ugly" mechanics work on the inside. The exterior seams work because the carbon fiber is folder back to the inside and fastened together and by the interior pieces. The bulbous forms are supported by the core of the interior. The interior is basically an engine where you circulate through some main large central spaces that connect you to many smaller spaces around it. This building gives you two different experiences; one on the outside and one inside.

AMAZON EXCHANGE: VISIONS FOR HQ2 IN LONG ISLAND CITY, QUEENS
Marion Weiss
Michael Manfredi (Guest Critic)
Eric Bellin (TA)

Graham Chair Professor of
Architecture, Co-founder of
Weiss/Manfredi, Recipient of
Academy Award in Architecture
from the American Academy
of Arts and Letters, the
Architectural League of New
York's Emerging Voices Award
and the New York AIA Gold M

CRITIC: MARION WEISS

After much speculation, and bids entertained from 238 American cities, Amazon has announced Long Island City, NY and Cristal City, VA as dual sites for the expansion of their corporate headquarters. This plan has, of course, both critics and champions. In New York, some condemn the deal as a waste of taxpayer money—the state has promised the company more than $500 million for construction, $1.2 billion in tax breaks, and $1.3 billion in other incentives. Others see it as a boon for NY, as Amazon plans to spend "$3.7 billion to build four to eight million square feet of office space—the equivalent of One World Trade Center two or three times over—for 25,000 workers in ten years, and possibly another 15,000 in the following five years." Whatever the case, Amazon's presence in Long Island City will, without doubt, disrupt its urban landscape.

Recent campus designs—such as those of Apple and Facebook in California—have been criticized as insular, closing themselves off from their surrounding contexts. The recent "Amazon Spheres," a set of interconnected biodomes on their Seattle campus, offer a visual symbol of environmental aspiration and agenda, but they remain closed to the public. But what if we challenge Amazon to offer a civic equivalent? In what ways can Amazon's new campus be cast not as a hermetically sealed box, but as a distributed network? And, as multinational corporations increasingly build large swathes of city, what gifts might they provide the public realm? Asking such questions, this studio seeks to offer visions for Amazon's Long Island City headquarters which stich themselves into the urban fabric, and propose paradigmatic and prototypical solutions for rethinking the connection between private corporation and public city.

RESEARCH AGENDA
This studio will be initiated with a four-week research project investigating case studies in three categories. Students will investigate multinational corporate campuses, identifying, studying, and critiquing existing paradigms. Multitasking infrastructures (bridges, transportation hubs, megastructures, etc.) and multivalent grounds (layered public spaces, landform buildings, etc.) will also be analyzed, offering precedents in catalyzing interconnection and exchange within urban environments.

DISRUPTING AND CONSTRUCTING THE EDGE
The planned site of Amazon's headquarters is situated along New York's East River. Rendering the research case studies—multinational corporate campuses, multitasking infrastructures, and multivalent grounds—operative in their design projects, students will be asked to articulate relationships across a number of edges: between land and water, interior and exterior, above and below, private company and public life, Manhattan and Queens.

FIELD WORK: NEW YORK
To understand the context and its varied opportunities, the studio will travel to Long Island City in Queens, NY and some of its surrounding areas. Additionally, a series of relevant precedent projects will be visited.

AMAZON EXCHANGE: VISIONS FOR HQ2 IN LONG ISLAND CITY, QUEENS

Marion Weiss

Jiacheng Gu, Zhen Meng

Our design is driven by an urban context, it consists of two main parts. One part is the landform building which extends into the city, the other part is two U-shaped buildings which float on the landscape as an icon.

The site is located at the border of Long Island City and Manhattan and is located by the East River, Roosevelt Island and Manhattan can be directly seen from here. Therefore, the building is composed of two u-shaped buildings, one facing the city and the other facing water. We extend the water system and landform building into the city, and at the same time remain the original network of the city road, allowing it to pass through the building and preserve the integrity of the urban road network to the greatest extent. Pedestrians in the city can directly enter the site from various points connecting the city. There are three different flows in our design, pedestrians can walk through the landscape or rooftop of the bar by following the city roads, or step directly into the buildings through the city. The interconnection of these three flows allows people to freely convert to the other flows in the building. In addition, the area around the site will be exposed to flooding. In this way, our design utilizes elements from Khaju Bridge, so it can resist the flood. The question we've been trying to think about in our design is what our design can offer the city beyond just being an Amazon Headquarter. Therefore, we provide maker space for new entrepreneurs in the city, some infrastructure for citizens, and also, we create a public park for the city.

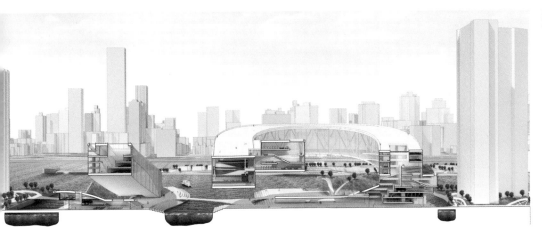

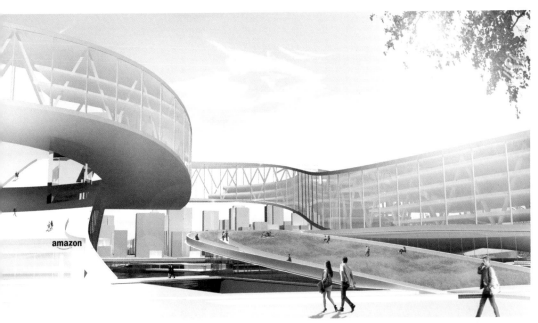

AMAZON EXCHANGE: VISIONS FOR HQ2 IN LONG ISLAND CITY, QUEENS

Marion Weiss

CRITIC: MARION WEISS

Riwan Heim, Ian Pangburn

As metropoles like New York City see an explosion in development, the demand for land speculation near urban cores takes precedent over questions of climate insecurity, socio-economic isolation and the nature of public space in our cities. Proposals like the Amazon HQ2 in Long Island City should call into question the way our field perceives high dollar investment in city space asking, "Where is the exchange in Amazon Exchange?" This proposal is one of many case studies interrogating this question and seeking new possibilities in the way architecture, city planning, and landscape can fuse existing and speculative networks together into a topographic Urban Tapestry.

THESIS
by Annette Fierro, Coordinator

In the final semester of the Master of Architecture program, each year a small group of honors students elect to pursue their thesis as an opportunity to undertake critical and speculative exploration. Building an independent topic or set of questions, they work closely with an advisor and collegial group of students and faculty over the course of the entire academic year. The thesis project is conceptualized as an open work, that is, its scope is limited only by the parameters of the questions posed. The question, the thesis topic, is necessarily a disciplinary challenge, establishing a relationship to ideas formally or popularly identified as architectural, whether belonging to the realm of building or the multiple discourses embraced within the discipline. Conversely, however, the thesis is also typically the site where students embracing dual degrees in Landscape Architecture, City Planning, and Historic Preservation choose to embody the final cross-disciplinary possibilities of their different subjects of study. Through the year-long thesis process, these questions are concurrently researched, elaborated, edited, and finally manifested in a work of architectural dimension. A thesis project is a work of craft, building a set of ideas into a final statement and set of conclusions.

The thesis project is also essentially timely: questions are posed to address current issues and crises in which architecture is implicated, even while often drawing on historical matter. In 2018-19, nine thesis projects addressed the extremes of contemporary subject matter: from questions of suburbia in the face of changing economic conditions (Kurt Nelson) and practices of commercial mass-generation (Lillian Candela), to questions prompted by specific cultural moments: strategies of developing affordable housing in post-Soviet Tbilisi (Irena Wight), the housing of stolen, cultural artifacts appropriated during recent periods of war in the middle east (Lauren Aguilar), to responses to pervasive forms of mass surveillance and potential shelter from them (Prince Langley). Several thesis projects also hinge on contemporary speculations which are technological, from the potential effect of highly responsive material systems on the essence of dwelling (Elizabeth Heldridge), to a speculated timeline of ecological infrastructure in times of marine crisis (Farre Nixon). All of the issues lie at the periphery but also comprise the centrality of architecture's role and responsibility within and crossing the boundaries of the discipline.

MASTER OF ARCHITECTURE THESIS
Advisors: Winka Dubbeldam and Frank Matero

Lauren Aguilar

Though very different institutions, the Met, the Getty, and US Immigration and Customs have a striking similarity in one regard. Each holds unmatched collections of antiquities. They focus efforts on study, acquisition, and object transfer. However, the Met and the Getty are renowned museums and ICE recovers and repatriates black market goods, keeping their collection in several top-secret warehouses. One such warehouse in Queens houses over 2,500 seized artifacts including "a huge stone Buddha from India, terra-cotta horsemen from China, reliefs from Iraq, Syria, and Yemen." Unlike the carefully curated collections at institutions like the Met, these pieces are a wildly varying group of rescues. These looted "parts" become displaced from their site or museum context and either disappear into private collections or spend years in government facilities awaiting repatriation.

In parallel globally and in the United States, the means and methods of war have greatly evolved leaving a vast aging building stock of military orphans. Traditional building typologies including munitions storage, forts, and bunkers have been superseded but are expensive or difficult to demolish. In addition, these spaces are crafted around defensive, introverted narratives.

A Safe House for Orphan Parts posits the role of architecture in repatriation and speculates on the proposed relationship between the orphan part and the orphaned building. The project seeks to explore the architectural opportunities to tell the story of looting in relation to terrorism.

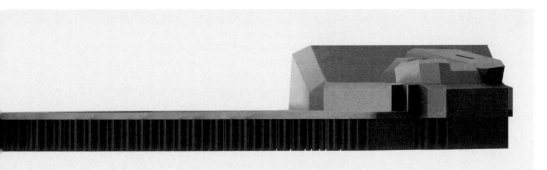

MASTER OF ARCHITECTURE THESIS
Advisor: Annette Fierro

CRITIC: ANNETTE FIERRO

Elizabeth Anne Heldridge

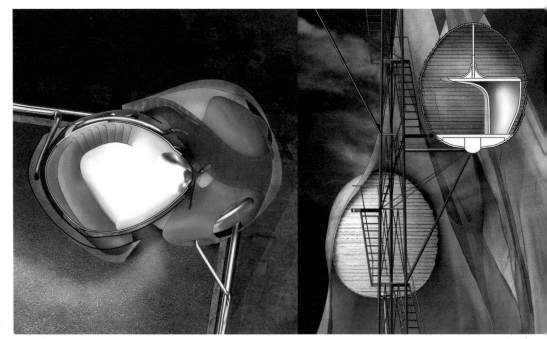

"Membrane" is a term which has historically been used to describe surface architecture or a glazed facade, with connotations of lightness, fragility, and transparency inherent in the term. As both a central topic of architectural history/theory as well as a highly popular building material, an exploration of membrane in these terms can feel limited. Epidermic Space speculates that through a reconsideration of membrane architecture, and in an analysis of natural and biological precedent, it may be possible to move beyond bubbles and glass and into new terrain.

These speculations have led to the design of a series of four "Experimental Bothies," sited within the formerly industrial Callowhill neighborhood in Northern Philadelphia. Each bothy is sited in a precise location that provides the environmental stimulus for which it is designed. And, within each of the four bothies, unique Epidermic Spaces expand beyond the physical edges of their thresholds to establish paradoxical relationships between bodily experience of the transient dweller and the fluctuating micro-climate within which the bothy exists.

The questions which guided this thesis are as follows:
- How can architectural thresholds—such as the window, door, and/or building envelope—mediate the relationships between built space, the environment, and experience of the inhabitant in an urban context?
- If space is understood as a biological membrane—at once providing separation and permeability—in which ways could this impact the experience of dwelling?
- How might a reconsideration of threshold as membrane inform a different programmatic understanding of urban dwellings, blurring the distinction between various types of internal or external space?
- Rather than a mere exposing of an interior environment to external stimulus such as wind, sound, heat, or humidity, are there ways in which these membranes could redirect or translate these experiences from one sensorial medium to another?

MASTER OF ARCHITECTURE THESIS
Advisors: Robert Stuart-Smith, Masoud Akbarzadeh, Karen M'Closkey

Farre Nixon

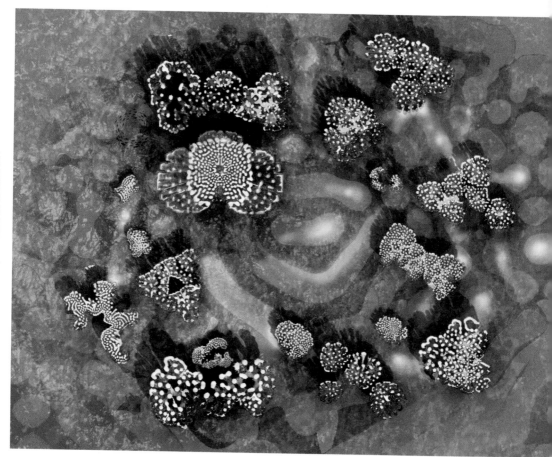

As the devastating effects of climate change continue to unfold upon the global environmental and socioeconomic stages, the need for direct intervention under new paradigms is clear. As the 2018 report issued by the Intergovernmental Panel on Climate Change implores, humanity must collectively act immediately to avoid the irreversible calamities that climate change holds in store.

Given the urgency of this situation, this thesis invites designers to venture under the sea to meet climate change at the frontlines. The research centers around corals: their morphology, physiology, role in healthy ecosystems, degradation due to anthropogenic activities, and potential for rehabilitation through innovative strategies that building and landscape architects wield within their purview.

The research adopts the radical approach of decentering the human and considering the needs of both human and non-human equally, culminating into a design proposal for an artificial reef archipelago that is capable of sustaining both constituents. The amorphous prosthesis hosts coral reefs that will acclimate and adapt to new climatic conditions, simultaneously creating a variety of micro-habitats ideal for coral reproduction and growth.

The project utilizes design fiction as the prevailing methodology to speculate on the viability, evolution, and influence of the artificial reef over time, from year 2020 to year 2100.

GALLERY

izabeth Anne Heldridge
ritic: Annette Fierro

Xu Yao and Long Ye
Critic: Joe MacDonald

Andrew Matia and Daniel Silverman
Critic: Georgina Huljich

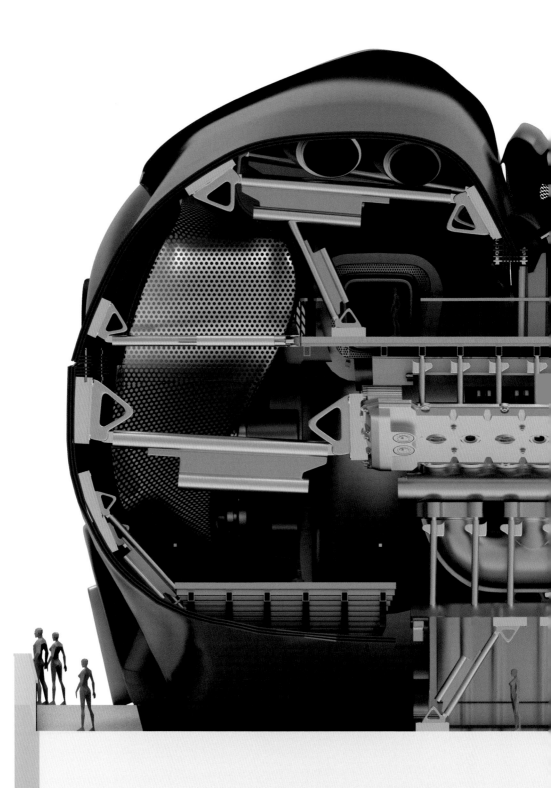

Luciano Najem and Ayotunde Ogunmoyero
Critic: Ali Rahim

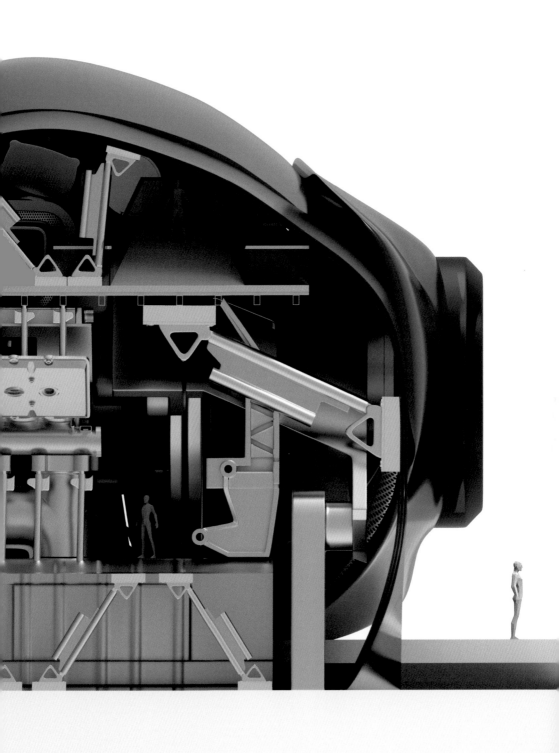

Zihao Fang, Bowen Qin, Weimeng Zhang
Critic: Simon Kim

AD
NC

NEW YORK CITY GATEWAY: A NEW PASSENGER AND CARGO TERMINAL FOR JOHN FITZGERALD KENNEDY AIRPORT, QUEENS, NEW YORK

Ezio Blasetti, Brian Deluna, Nate Hume, Ali Rahim,
TAs: Carrie Frattali, Angela Huang, Angeliki Tzifa, Caleb White

This studio explored design techniques and the history of New York City's architecture and combined it with an understanding of global capital markets to develop a new Airport/Distribution Center Hub for New York City.

NEW YORK CITY FINANCIAL LEADERSHIP CHALLENGED

In times of immense growth in capital due to economies in China, India, and the Middle East including the UAE and Qatar there is more capital than ever in the world today. While monetary capital has always played a significant role in determining the built environment, recent shifts in the character of global finance have resulted in a new relationship between investment practices and buildings. This fact has resulted in 14 pencil towers that are planned or under construction in Manhattan. The fact that Manhattan has served as the receptor of global capital has maintained its status as a global leader. Now the city is exhausted with an oversupply of new condominiums. An example is 53 W 53rd Street designed by Jean Nouvel that came to market in September 2015 and is only 55 percent sold today. With its financial leadership being challenged by other cities including London, Dubai, Hong Kong and Tokyo how will New York respond to this challenge?

Financial capitals need strong economies and economies are changing rapidly across the world. The triumvirate of easy money, cheap imports and strong confidence catalyze growth in Western economies. New York City's financial global leadership has been sustained by the culmination of all three. Today these are coming to an end, interest rates are increasing, low cost retailers such as American Apparel and Radio Shack have filed for bankruptcy, and an uncertain political climate have shaken confidence in the US economy. All three components have threatened New York City as the Global financial capital.

AIRPORTS

More specifically, this studio speculates that a new airport typology can help sustain New York City's financial global leadership in the world. To maintain its leadership, export opportunities to and in developing economies are more likely to fuel growth. In addition there are new opportunities driven by technology and growth opportunities in the emerging markets. Long haul flights are needed and there is an increased demand from travelers flying to Asia and other emerging markets. Airports should negotiate these growth opportunities with more luxurious and efficient travel experiences. At the same time the rise of a technologically driven retail giants such as Amazon uses distribution networks that channel materials and goods to remote locations that are delivered through existing delivery networks including DHL, USPS, UPS and FedEx. Price Water-house Coopers indicates that currently 90 percent of global trade flows through 39 airports and states that global trade is set to increase rapidly. The city's that become the most important of these gateway regions will thrive. US retail will benefit with an efficient hub accessible directly from New York City establishing it as the leader of cargo nationally and internationally. Currently JFK is ranked 16th in the world with the number of travelers that move through the airport each year and 21st in cargo traffic. Other cities vying for global leadership are ranked much higher in passenger and cargo traffic. Hong Kong, Tokyo, and Dubai are all in the top 8 in both passenger and cargo traffic. The airport terminal that deals with passengers and cargo will contribute towards reducing the disparity between cities vying for financial global leadership and New York City. The

w terminal will increase the relevance of JFK as a business and logistics
b making a stronger connection to global centers and strengthening devel-
ment locally.

ARCHITECTURE: TWO HISTORIES,
NEW YORK CITY AND LONG SPAN STRUCTURES

the history of the development of Manhattan with the growth of the
y, by means of laying a grid over vast territory, architecture becomes
e expression of capital due to its increase of land value. The land value of
nhattan was generated by modes of densification of building mass. Within
e beginning of "the liberal city" architecture becomes the outcome of
tical expressions based on its relationship to its land. The hypothesis of
e studio is to speculate on the idea that architecture incorporated
ments of the city to increase its value. In the 19th century the incorporation
the land into the building by the repetition of floors and in the beginning
the 20th century an interest in aesthetic styles into order to express
e building as a mode of commerce, then within the '30s the Skyscraper
orporated the whole city under one roof. To search for a new typology, it
l mean that we turn the building away from its means as solely for human
abitation and understand the project as a means of generating capital
rough the exchange of goods. The thesis taken within the studio is that
e Architecture of the airport strengthens New York City's value by fusing
ban elements into a new form of architectural interiority, while strengthening
e financial leadership in the world.

As we re-think the typology of the airport we will also explore the four
es of long span structures that use tensile and compressive forces. The
r types we will investigate through the course of the term are form that
lude cable and pneumatic structures, section that include framed and
b structures, vector that include multi-dimensional splitting structures
d surface that includes folded and shell structures. The history has been
extensive one that started with single level spaces the Pantheon being
e of the earliest (118-128), the Hagia Sophia (532-537) St. Peters Cathedral
06-1615). Crystal Palace was built in 1851 that used cast iron and plate
ss. Later in 1870 the first passenger elevator was used in the Equitbe Life
ilding in New York City which propelled the typology of the skyscraper.
th the invention of the skyscraper, the long span structure took on a
ferent form that intersects the history of the long span structures with
pital pushing towards the limits of engineering. In the same manner we will
estigate the long span typology to form the basis of our understanding to
ent new structural and spatial typologies that are appropriate for the
w typology of the Gateway.

A GATEWAY FOR PASSENGERS AND CARGO,
JAMAICA, QUEENS. NEW YORK CITY

e site is at John F Kennedy Airport. In particular we are designing a new
teway Hub which is the entry sequence to the airport and combining it
h a cargo terminal developing a new typology for New York City's airports.
K is uniquely equipped to speculate on the Gateway Hub into a precise
d novel architecture and urban proposal that are unprecedented that links
bal and local conditions.

NEW YORK CITY GATEWAY
Ezio Blasetti, Brian Deluna, Nate Hume, Ali Rahim

Cai Zhang, Yuan Zhang, Yiling Zhong

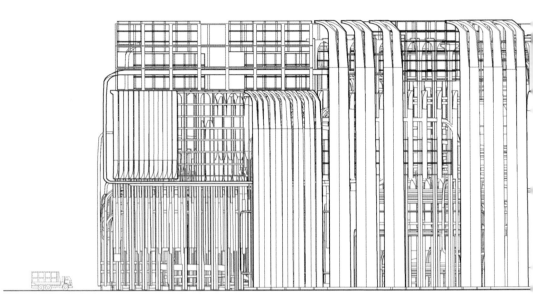

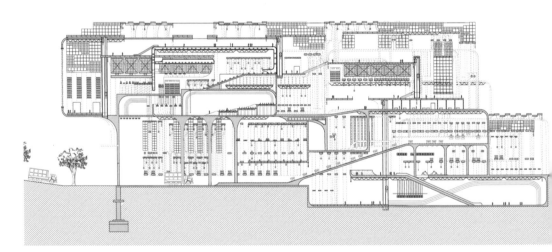

Our project is composed of basic frame units just like our precedent Pompidou, structure units assembled together and make a free space for all kinds of activities. In our project, different sizes of frame units combined and intertwined into a complex transmission logistics system. In the building, the cargo is transported by conveyor belts and suspended robots. We designed many layers of pipes and conveyor belts and each layer of pipeline is responsible for the transportation of a certain warehouse cargo. When the frame is closely arranged without gaps, a flat space is provided for people's activities like check-in and check-out. The shelves are combined with the conveyor belt, and connect different frames in different height, which stabilizes the structure and makes the storage space more flexible.

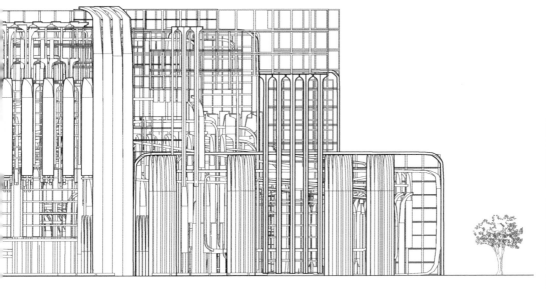

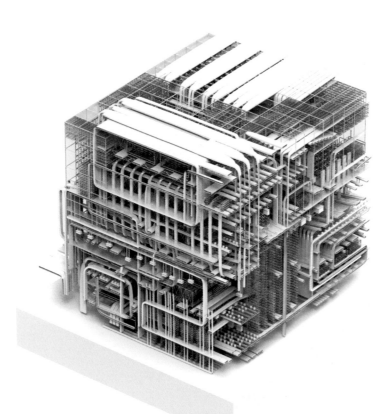

NEW YORK CITY GATEWAY
Ezio Blasetti, Brian Deluna, Nate Hume, Ali Rahim

Zhen Meng, Hao Zeng

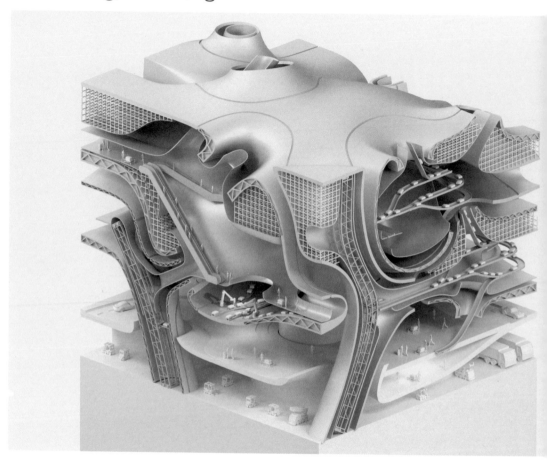

Our project is derived from the relationship between curves. When curves are infinitely close to the control lines, adjacent areas centered on the intersection of the lines begins to change. The curves begin to move closer and squeeze each other. In this way, we are focusing on what kinds of continuous and changing space will be created by such changes. From the interacting curved lines, we turned the plane into a three-dimensional model to let the line become the surface of the boundary and space, shape becomes volume. Then we combine and arrange these prototypes in a larger scale to find what kind of space and boundaries does these modules create. We cut each module to expose its spatial properties, to rotate and nest each module, thus, we produced multiple layers during the composition process so that there are many gap spaces between these layers. There are multiple inner and outer surfaces that can be transformed into each other. Besides, while combining these module, we also introduce four different scales. In this way, the combination of layers becomes freer and more flexible.

Flat surfaces are designed for humans to move besides the surfaces, and the space between smoother and more flexible surfaces are used for logistics. The openings in each module is use for many type of functions. The openings at the bottom of the building is used as columns, space for elevations, and space for escalators. The other openings at the surface or the top of the building are used as windows and light well.

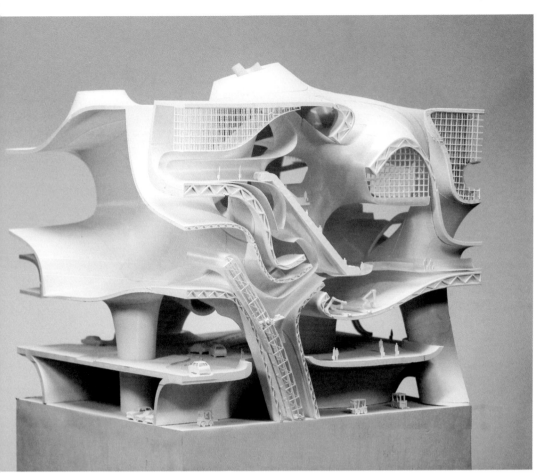

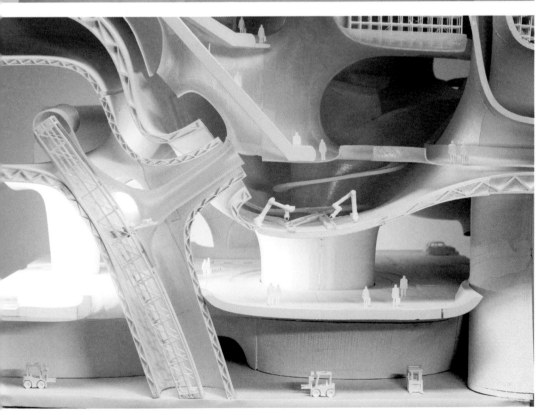

REMAPPING THE ENERGY FIELD: CLIMATE-RESPONSIVE DESIGN WITHIN THE CONTEMPORARY CITY
Dorit Aviv
Kit Elsworth (TA)

Ph.D Candidate: Princeton University, M.Arch: Princeton University, B.Arch: The Cooper Union

CRITIC: DORIT AVIV

Our objective is to explore what it means to Design with Climate. How do we create an architecture that harnesses environmental forces towards its own performance as a shelter for human inhabitation on a specific site? Our understanding of climate within an urban setting should also integrate the impact of human-made environments on local heating and thermal comfort.

The city is a territory of multiple diverse microclimates, each a site for thermodynamic interactions where energy flows are in constant exchange with human-made structures. Through these interactions, the magnitudes of forces such as radiation or convection are enhanced and multiplied or, conversely, subdued dramatically. A specific urban microclimate is therefore the dynamic reciprocal action between naturally occurring global cycles and their interface with urban canyons and skyscrapers, concrete roads and reflective-glass curtain walls. From the perspective that any design decision will inherently intervene on this energy field, in this studio we will seek to redefine the architectural design procedure in the city. First, we will use dynamic software tools and physical modeling to map the forces affecting a site. Second, we will intervene on these newly mapped and visualized energy flows through architectural design. This workflow offers a critique of black-box simulations, in which the results are disassociated from the procedure that produced them. Instead, we will explore how the simulation and modeling tools we utilize to process the data and how we can intentionally manipulate the calculated acting forces with our tool palette. The goal is to break down the black box into its components and therefore be able to intervene on it.

In the second part of the semester, program and typology are introduced. A prototype for an urban workspace is to be developed for each of the microclimates investigated in the first part of the studio. The program will combine indoor and outdoor spaces for gathering and individual work. The design procedure will explore new ways of thinking about the common urban typology of the office building in light of the demands we face today as architects to respond to both the environment and the needs of the people occupying the space. As a first step a typological study will be conducted to gain insight into how the building massing, form and orientation affect local comfort.

Next, we will explore how the human body interacts with its surroundings through the mitigation of architectural elements that are adaptive to changing external and internal forces. Because both external climate and internal metabolic rate are variable over time, the building environment should not be understood as a steady state comfort-machine but rather as a producer of multiple transitory states throughout day-night cycles and seasonal changes. Each microclimate requires its own set of bioclimatic design strategies. In turn, these strategies affect the urban environments around them. The energy field emerging from these interventions will be iteratively re-mapped, to reflect the consequences of design proposals when projected back into the city.

ADVANCED" 708 [MEBD]

REMAPPING THE ENERGY FIELD: CLIMATE-RESPONSIVE DESIGN WITHIN THE CONTEMPORARY CITY

Dorit Aviv

Shibei Huang, Uroosa Ijaz

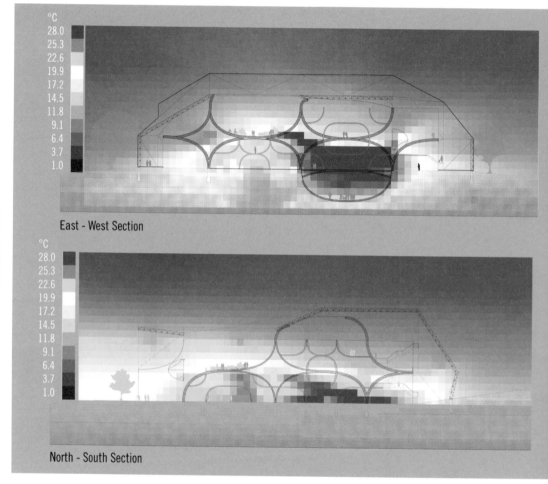

East - West Section

North - South Section

Salt Lake City is in a climate 5B zone, on the edge of zone 6, indicating a cold and dry climate. Its unique geographical location merits careful analysis into its nuanced climate at multiple scales. First, the siting of the city between two mountain ranges on the east and west coupled with lakes on the north and south mark the city a valley. On a regional scale (a comparison with the closest cities across either mountain ranges), the valley retains and releases heat slower indicating warmer winters and cooler summers. Other climatic factors studied include wind velocity at the base of the mountain ranges, and soil conductivities. Shoebox studies of various typologies with their respective energy loads is presented as the first step to understanding how different forms and materials respond to the climate.

The culmination of this research lead to a 50,000-sf office building that relies on passive strategies from the environment to sustain indoor comfort. The first move is to create layers of program requiring different thermal comfort in the logic of thermal onion (see diagram). The second design decision is to use geothermal energy, circulating underground water in the surfaces in the 'cores', where the most condition program reside. By embedding the heat in winter and coolth in summer, the building is projected to achieve thermal comfort by minimal active system.

REMAPPING THE ENERGY FIELD: CLIMATE-RESPONSIVE DESIGN WITHIN THE CONTEMPORARY CITY

Dorit Aviv

Chunyi Wang, Liang Zhang, Yunwen Zhu

CRITIC: DORIT AVIV

By overlaying GIS-detected heat island hot spots in Philadelphia with the regional topography, urban density, vegetation, and industry, we found the combination of factors contributing to the phenomenon. Based on these findings, our design aimed to mitigate the heat island effect in a hot spot we detected around city hall square. City hall square and Love Park are significant public outdoor spaces in Philadelphia. However, the heat island phenomenon renders this urban space uncomfortable for people to enjoy the city landmarks during the summer. In our project, we aimed to create a comfortable outdoor plaza in both winter and summer by self-shading and working with the strong wind from the direction of the Benjamin Franklin Pkwy. Our project consists of an office tower and a landscaped plaza with particular gardens for summer and winter. The plaza's terrain was formed to create a wind shadow in one area and increase wind speed in another area. Based on topological analysis of radiation, ray-tracing, and wind velocity, the original tower massing was carved by natural forces. Double façade was also implemented, with three different geometries to mitigate high, medium, and low radiation.

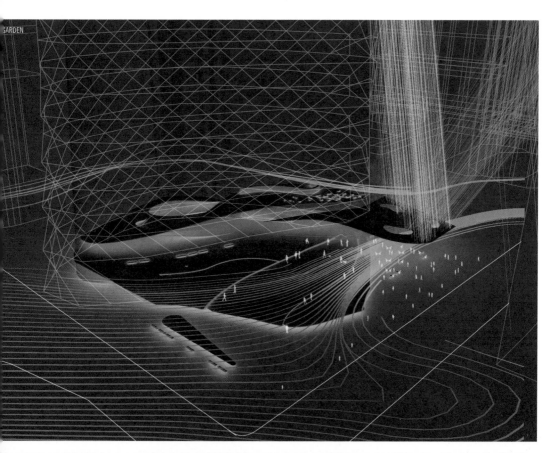

ADVANCED" 708 [MEBD]

DOCTORAL DEGREE

by Daniel Barber, Associate Professor and Chair of the
Graduate Group in Architecture

The Graduate Group in Architecture offers Ph.D degrees focus on advanced
research in architecture and landscape architecture. While students focus
on history/theory or technology, the program is especially interested in
interdisciplinary scholarship that pushes the boundaries of these disciplines
and their inter-related research trajectories. Student projects often explore
connections between architectural histories and theories and histories of
technology and environment; of race, class, and gender; of politics, economics,
and equity; many are attuned to the role of media in producing and understanding architectural ideas. Research in structures, performance, and
robotics are also informed by a robust engagement with pressing social
and environmental issues.

   The program is based on the premise that advanced research in the field
is essential to adjusting the content of and context for architectural ideas
and practices. This is not simply a means to produce new narratives, or
elaborate on technological possibilities; we aim to ask questions that reconsider the relationship between design and cultural value, and that assess
how architecture and landscape architecture engage and rearrange existing
frameworks of social and political life.

   Students produce written work that is at the leading edge of the field;
Ph.Ds also become teachers, and take this responsibility to the discipline,
and its ever-changing parameters, into academic and professional positions,
as well as to conferences, symposia, lectures, and other discussions. Some
examples of current research projects follow, please explore the Ph.D website
for more details.

DOCTORAL DEGREE PROGRAM
Advisor: David Leatherbarrow

Liyang Ding

Hans Scharoun and China: The Role of Chinese Urban and Cosmological Culture in Scharoun's "Aperspectival" Space

This dissertation aims to provide a critical account of an understudied and yet important connection between East and West in the history of modern architecture, namely, Hans Scharoun and China. The history of the "Chinese Werkbund" has been documented, with a focus on Hugo Häring's and Chen Kuan Lee's encounters with East Asian architecture and culture. But the significance of Chinese culture for Scharoun cannot be denied, even if it has been neglected to date. Particularly, Scharoun's intensive study of Chinese urban and cosmological culture and his later applications of pertinent concepts to architecture remain largely unknown. Further investigation is therefore necessary, to understand Scharoun's work, his evolving conception of architectural space, and Asian-European exchange in modern architecture. By examining the archival evidence that suggests Scharoun's debt to Chinese culture, this research answers the following questions: what motivated Scharoun's enduring interest in China, what is the relationship between his "organic" approach—inaugurated by Hermann Muthesius and further developed by Häring and Scharoun—and the Chinese parallel, and, more importantly, how did Scharoun's study of China affect the formation and development of his spatial conception and urban vision in his postwar practice, both formally and conceptually. The main thesis of my dissertation is that, resulting from the critique of the historical-cultural presuppositions—the geometric conception of space and the prolonged interest in perspective for spatial construction—of both Western architecture and modern science during the past two centuries, Scharoun's encounter with Chinese culture reinforced and clarified his all-encompassing architectural thinking, ranging from "aperspectival" space, to his "organic" design approach, as well as to his "city-landscape" and "collective plan" urban visions.

erman Pallares

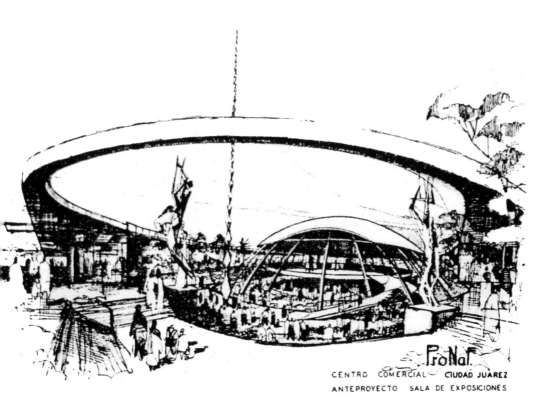

CENTRO COMERCIAL CIUDAD JUAREZ
ANTEPROYECTO SALA DE EXPOSICIONES

e on the Border: Constructing the México/US Borderland
om 1961 to 1971

e on the Border interprets the urban projects of the 1960s in the México/US
rderland as agents of modernization. It reveals them as projections of
e socioeconomic and cultural policies that characterized the relations
the United States with México during the Cold War. The dissertation
alyzes the evolution of the border cities through major governmental
ojects at different scales and their perception on both sides of the border.
ocuses on the Mexican 1961 Programa Nacional Fronterizo/ National
rder Program [PRONAF], and the 1964 Programa de Industrialización
la Frontera/ Border Industrialization Program [PIF], that proposed models
economic and cultural development through the construction of modern
perblocks in the major border twin-cities. It contrasts the Mexican initiatives
at prioritized cultural exchange with the efforts of the American
vernment that focused mainly on connective infrastructure. The study
ngs to light the architecture and infrastructure of the binational
terprises as local responses to global conflicts.

Rui B. de Morais e Castro

Transgressive Transparency
Dan Graham Pavilions, Art/Architecture, and the Public in the Long 1970s

This dissertation contributes to debates on the potential of art and architecture and of their relationship to shape the public as a category within a democratic society. It places as its central object the work of the American artist Dan Graham, an agent that since the mid-1960s to today, illuminates and shapes those debates in crucial ways. It explains how Dan Graham became Dan Graham, the artist of the more than 70 two-way mirror-glass pavilions built in the whole world since the late 1970s. The dissertation shows that the pavilions are tools to address audiences beyond the art world and to induce in individuals a form of self-reflection that prompted an understanding of their own subjectivity in the context of late modernity and technological change. Moreover, appropriating the architectural language of glass construction, these pavilions also act as a critique of corporate architecture culture and its illusions of transparency and "democracy." Functioning ludically, they allow audiences to experiment with—and literally reflect upon—glass architecture as a vehicle of spectacle and alienation. In a world in which glass architecture and digital screens are ubiquitous, the critical power of Graham's pavilions is only amplified.

ang Pil Lee

anded Environments: Arata Isozaki and Hans Hollein, Architects of the
and Media in the First Electronic Age, 1955–1976

s dissertation examines architects' endeavors to create new living envi-
ments during the postwar period that corresponded to new modes of
king developed by discourse on media and communications in association
electric and electronic technology. It focuses, in particular, on how the
dern concept of space was challenged, diversified, and finally re-conceptualized
environmental conceptions in architecture within the discourse on the
and, as a result, how the notion of environments and cities became, in
tain decisive contexts, interchangeable. Rather than seeking to find a
gle origin for this transformation, this research investigates a constellation
nterrelated theories including Gestalt psychology, cybernetics, and
shall McLuhan's media theory, and their influences on postwar urbanism
architecture. To trace the impact of the circulation of these theories in
inct national contexts, it particularly analyzes the theoretical and design
eavors of architects in Vienna represented by Hans Hollein and Tokyo by
ta Isozaki. This dissertation argues that these architects employed the
ve-mentioned theories to dismantle modern architectural concepts such
pace and form as well as to reconceptualize architecture as a means of
vating human life. The result was the development of a shared concept
he expanded environment: one that stimulates social consciousness and
ws people to communicate and to conduct their social affairs through
tric media.

CO
SE

URS

COURSE DESCRIPTIONS

ARCH 511
History and Theory I
Joan Ockman — 2018C

The century between the Crystal Palace and Lever House witnessed the emergence of a dramatically new building culture with far-reaching consequences. In this overview of international architecture from the second half of the nineteenth century through the first half of the twentieth, we will situate the icons and isms, the pioneers and hero figures within a broad technological, economic, sociopolitical, and cultural context. The thirteen lectures will move both chronologically and thematically, tracing architecture's changing modes of production and reception; its pivotal debates, institutions, and tendencies; and its expanding geography, highlighting the ways the culture of architecture responded to and mediated the unprecedented experiences of modernity. We will also reflect on modernism's legacy today. The objective of the course is not just to acquaint students with seminal buildings and their architects but also to foster a strong understanding of history and of architecture's place in a modernizing world. Readings drawn from primary and secondary literature as well as a recently published text that is among the first to place modern architecture into a global perspective will supplement the lectures and provide a rich introduction to the historiography of the hundred-year period.

ARCH 512
History and Theory II
Sophie Hochhäusl — 2019A

This course traces the emergence of contemporary issues in the field by exploring the architecture of the twentieth century. Buildings, projects, and texts are situated within the historical constellations of ideas, values, and technologies that inform them through a series of close readings. Rather than presenting a parade of movements or individuals, the class introduces topics as overlaying strata, with each new issue adding greater complexity even as previous layers retain their significance. Of particular interest for the course is the relationship between architecture and the organizational regimes of modernity.

ARCH 521
Visual Studies I
Nathan Hume — 2018C

Visual Studies I is the engagement of graphic and visual information found in the world and in media, and its ability to contain—and more importantly, to convey—meaningful information. Intelligence in visual information is deployed to transfer cultural values, to educate and influence, and to create new relationships not easily expressed through mathematics, linguistics, and applied science.

One of the challenges in the course is the re-invention of a means of assessment, the development of notations and techniques that will document the forces and the production of difference in the spatial manifestations of the generative systems. Tactility, material, scale, profile, shape, color, Architecture works primarily in the assertion of these modes, and the meaningful production and control of these modes of communication are imperative for all designers.

ARCH 522
Visual Studies II
Nathan Hume — 2019A

Visual Studies II extends the use of the computer as a tool for architectural representation and fabrication by engaging in digital three-dimensional modeling. Modeling is approached first of all as a set of techniques for exploring and determining design intent and direction. Attention is given to precision and detailed modeling, paralleled by the development of the critical understanding for the constructive translation between physical and digital working environments.

This course analyzes the intensive and extensive properties at the scale of the city through a series of mapping exercises. Computational strategies of transformation are deployed to create explicit formations, by utilizing the analytical methods as generative procedures. The resulting systems become the basis for experimentation with computer aided manufacturing tools of the school. In parallel to the development of modeling skills, exercises in visualization emphasize both the analytic and affective possibilities of computer-generated imagery.

ARCH 531
Construction I
Philip Ryan — 2018C

This lecture course explores the basic principles of architectural technology and building construction. Focus is placed on building material, methods of on-site and off-site preparation, material assemblies, and the material performance. Topics discussed include load bearing masonry structures of small to medium size (typical row house construction), heavy and light wood frame construction, sustainable construction practices, emerging and engineered materials, and integrated building practices. The course also introduces students to Building Information Modeling (BIM) via the production of construction documents.

ARCH 532
Construction II
Franca Trubiano — 2019A

The course is focused on building materials, methods of on-site and off-site construction, architectural assemblies, and the performance of materials. A continuation of Construction I, focusing on light and heavy steel frame construction, concrete construction, light and heavyweight cladding systems and systems building.

ARCH 535
Structures I
Richard Farley,
Masoud Akbarzadeh — 2018C

Theory applied toward structural form. The study of static and hyperstatic systems and design of their elements. Flexural theory, elastic and plastic. Design for combined stresses; prestressing. The study of graphic statics and the design of trusses. The course comprises both lectures and a weekly laboratory in which various structural elements, systems, materials and technical principles are explored.

ARCH 536
Structures II
Richard Farley,
Masoud Akbarzadeh — 2019A

A continuation of the equilibrium analysis of structures covered in Structures I. A review one-dimensional structural elements; a stud of arches, slabs and plates, curved surface structures, lateral and dynamic loads; surve of current and future structural technology. The course comprises both lectures and a weekly laboratory in which various structura elements, systems, materials and technical principles are explored.

ARCH 611
History and Theory III
Daniel Barber, David Leatherbarrow, Sophie Hochhäusl, Stephen Anderson — 2018C

This is the third and final required course in t history and theory of architecture. It is a lect course that examines selected topics, figures, projects, and theories from the history of arc tecture and related design fields during the 20 century. The course also draws on related and parallel historical material from other discipli and arts, placing architecture into a broader socio-cultural-political-technological context.

ARCH 621
Visual Studies III
Nathan Hume — 2018C

The final of the Visual Studies half-credit courses. Drawings are explored as visual repositories of data from which information c be gleaned, geometries tested, designs refine and transmitted. Salient strengths of various digital media programs are identified and developed through assignments that address th specific intentions and challenges of the desig studio project.

ARCH 631
Tech Case Studies I
Lindsay Falck — 2018C

A study of the active integration of various building systems in exemplary architectural projects. To deepen students' understanding the process of building, the course compares the process of design and construction in buildings of similar type. The course brings forward the nature of the relationship betwee architectural design and engineering systems and highlights the crucial communication skills required by both the architect and the engineer.

ARCH 633
Environmental Systems I
Dorit Aviv — 2018C

In the spring portion of Environmental System we consider the environmental systems of larger, more complex buildings. Contemporary buildings are characterized by the use of systems such as ventilation, heating, cooling, dehumidification, lighting, communications, an controls that not only have their own demand

interact dynamically with one another.
r relationship to the classic architectural
stions about building size and shape are
n more complex. With the introduction of
nisticated feedback and control systems,
nitects are faced with conditions that are
ually animate and coextensive at many
es with the natural and man-made environ-
ts in which they are placed.

ARCH 634
Environmental Systems II
zabeth Escott — 2019A

s course considers the environmental
cems of larger, more complex buildings.
temporary buildings are characterized by
use of systems such as ventilation, heating,
ing, dehumidification, lighting, communica-
s, and controls that not only have their
demands, but interact dynamically with
another. Their relationship to the classic
nitectural questions about building size and
pe are even more complex. With the intro-
tion of sophisticated feedback and control
cems, architects are faced with conditions
t are virtually animate and coextensive at
y scales with the natural and man-made
ronments in which they are placed.

ARCH 636
Material Formations
bert Stuart-Smith — 2019A

erial Formations introduces robotic pro-
tion and material dynamics as active agents
esign rationalization and expression. The
rse investigates opportunities for designers
ynthesize multiple performance criteria
in architecture. Technical theory, case-
dies, and practical tutorials will focus on
rporation of simulation, generative compu-
n, and robot fabrication concerns within
gn. While production is traditionally viewed
n explicit and final act of execution, the
rse explores the potential for all aspects of
ding production to participate within the
ative design process, potentially producing
formance and affect. Students will develop
s and experience in computer program-
g, physics-based simulation, and robot
ion planning. A design research project will
ndertaken through a number of discrete
gnments that requires a design synthesis
ween form and material considerations
gside robotic production constraints. The
rse will explore design as the outcome of
erially formative processes of computation
production.

ARCH 671
Professional Practice I
ilip Ryan — 2019A

course consists of a series of workshops
introduce students to a diverse range
ractices. The course goal is to gain an
erstanding of the profession by using the
ect process as a framework. The course
prises a survey of the architectural profes-
- its licensing and legal requirements; its
ving types of practice, fees and compensa-
; its adherence to the constraints of codes
regulatory agencies, client desires and
gets; and its place among competing and
d professions and financial interests. The
kshops are a critical forum for discussion
nderstand the forces which at times both
ede and encourage innovation and leader-
. Students learn how architects develop
skills necessary to effectively communicate
lients, colleagues, and user groups. Trends
n as globalization, ethics, entrepreneurship,
cainability issues and technology shifts are
yzed in their capacity to affect the practice
architect.

ARCH 710
Contemporary Theory
1989—Present
Joan Ockman — 2018C

This course is an introduction to contemporary
architectural theory. The alphabet serves as
a heuristic device for organizing a list of inter-
related topics that have animated and informed
architectural discourse over the past three
decades. In previous periods theory offered
architects a set of principles and justifications
for their work. Today it functions more as a
mode of thought, a platform for debate, and
an array of critical strategies. The aim of the
course is to provide architecture students with
a toolkit for both cultural literacy and more
meaningful and engaged architectural practice.
As a collective project, the class will produce an
illustrated and annotated dictionary.

ARCH 711
Building Theories
Franca Trubiano — 2018C

Recent architectural projects have showcased
unprecedented building technologies and inven-
tions. The introduction of new materials, alternative energy sources, big data and the reorganiza-
tion of global labor practices, have redefined the
art of building. However, faced with these vast
transformations in how we design and practice,
architectural theory has been less than equipped
to discuss, evaluate, and debate their impact.
Required is the ability to analyze, rationalize, and
theorize their consequences; required is a theory
of BUILDING. For decades, architectural theory
has been remiss to recognize the contribution
which building practices have made to how we
'think' about architecture. Redressing this condition is the goal of this seminar; dedicated to the
critical examination of ideas fundamental to the
art of building. In a text-based review of both
significant contemporary projects and seminal
architectural writings, this seminar outlines the
first ideas of the nascent field that is Building
Theories. Designs require their construction,
and construction requires rationalization; and it
is in this reciprocity that students are invited to
elaborate a new theoretical field.

ARCH 711
Strange Symmetries:
Towards A Symmetrical
Architecture
David Salomon — 2018C

Allegedly exorcised in the 20th century for
its indifference to use, context and climate, it
never really disappeared. Today, it is back with a
vengeance. The diverse, if not divergent practices
that use symmetry include: Reiser + Umemoto,
MAD, Zaha Hadid, MOS, OMA, OFFICE, Foster,
Pezo von Ellrichshausen, Dogma, David Ruy, Mark
Foster Gage and Young + Ayata. Why symmetry,
why now? The seminar will look at the history of
symmetry as an idea, its use in architecture, and
its subsequent expansion into other intellectual
arenas. It will then turn its attention to current
debates within architectural discourse—namely,
those around flat-ontology, Object Oriented
Ontology, and global architectural history—and
the sublimated presence of symmetry within
them. Next, we will look at and compare historical
and contemporary architectural projects with
one another, using the presence of symmetry
in them to help identify/establish cross-cultural
and cross-temporal affinities and disjunctions
between them. Finally, the ideas of Latour,
DeLanda, Harman and others will be deployed
to theorize the return of symmetry. In short,
through the close examination of symmetrical
architecture and ideas about symmetry we will
ask if symmetry—with its exhibited capacity to
cross borders without losing its identity—help
architecture avoid having to make the false
choice between autonomy and engagement?

ARCH 711
Modern Architecture in
Japan: Culture, Place,
Tectonics
Ariel Genadt — 2018C

This seminar explores the diversity of forms
and meanings that modern architecture took
on in Japan since its industrialization in the
19th century. With this focus, it opens up
wider questions on the capacity of construction, materials and their assembly to express
and represent cultural, aesthetic, climatic and
social concerns. Rather than an exhaustive
chronological survey, the course demonstrates
salient topics and milestones in the country's
recent architectural history, and places them
in contexts of parallel practices in the world.
It examines drawings, images, texts and films
on architects whose work and words were
emblematic of each topic.

ARCH 711
Non-Cities
Paul Preissner — 2018C

Sometime around the 1970s market ideology
became the divine star for the redevelopment
of American and European cities. The domain
which was once considered thoroughly public
began ceding its territory to the private sector, often for very cheap. What was returned
was safety and security, what was taken was
unpredictability and freedom. Popular and
marketable again, cities compete with each
other for the affection of the world's elite tour-
ists and investors at the expense of their actual
residents. The effects of this redirection of urban space and the cultural outlines that make it
possible have developed a type of space, which
Auge' titles as the "non-space." Building off this
reading of social space that exists outside of
clarity and memory, this seminar extends the
designation to that of the city.

The city exists as one of the great projects
of humankind, simultaneously both conditioned
by people and conditioning of people. If today
the city is understand as vehicle for economies
and lifestyle, this seminar investigates the forms
of cities which exist outside the conventional
understanding of the global city. These are places
which cannot be understand as successes or failures according to the measurements of capital,
and therefore allow for new forms of order and
cultural relationships to occur.

This research seminar will be structured
to at first identify the contemporary definitions
of the city along with the recent paths which have
brought us here, and then detour through a set
of case studies to better understand alternative
urban forms. These case studies will allow us to
speculate on the limits of a city though differing
identifiers of "city-ness."

ARCH 711
Automation in Construction:
Architecture in the 4th and
5th Industrial Revolution
Anna Pla Català — 2018C

This course will research the potential of Auto-
mation in Construction (AC) within the technological and cultural paradigm opened up by the
4th and 5th Industrial Revolutions. Particular
focus will be placed on the latest developments
in Additive Manufacturing (AM) and Robotic

Fabrication (RF) applied to architectural construction at the building scale. Whether it is a singular component or a complete building, the full-scale fabrication capabilities of AC, AM and RF is today a fact that is revolutionising design practices and everyday construction

ARCH 712
Life on the Border: The Built Environment of Transboundary Urban Space
German Pallares — 2019A

This course considers the architecture that makes the borders of cities, regions, and nations. Case studies central to this course will include: the border shared between México and the United States, the Demilitarized Zone (DMZ) of North-South Korea, and the land dividing Palestinian and Israeli territories. Other examples, like the Berlin Wall, will be used as complimentary analogues. The seminar will critically assess how architecture has been leveraged to facilitate state and institutional control of space; but also, how architecture and it's projective tools like maps, plans, signage, and patterns of use can act as operative forces for alienation, segregation, division, violence and surveillance, as well as the post-border potential of architecture for connection, communication, and collaboration.

ARCH 712
Articulate Building Envelopes: Construction and Expression
Ariel Genadt — 2019A

In the 20th century, building envelopes have become the prime architectural subject of experimentations and investments, as well as physical failures and theoretical conflicts. This seminar examines the meaning of performance of 20th-century envelopes by unfolding their functions and behaviors in salient case studies, in practice and in theory. While the term performance is often used to denote quantifiable parameters, such as exchanges of energy, airs and waters, this seminar seeks to recouple these with other, simultaneous performances, which can be grouped under the term articulation. Albeit numbers cannot describe articulation, its consideration is key to the interpretation of quantifiable performances. Ultimately, the articulation of envelopes' polyvalence is the measure of their civic pertinence.

ARCH 712
Architectures of Refusal: On Spatial Justice in the South Bronx
Eduardo Rega — 2019A

A neighborhood with a remarkable history of struggle against inept municipal governments, neoliberalism and the forces behind the breeding of decay, the South Bronx is currently experiencing an aggressive wave of gentrification and policies that keep benefitting small elites. Grassroots organizations are fighting back while practicing radical imaginations for a more just future. Architectures of Refusal: On Spatial Justice in the South Bronx aims to reflect and develop collective architecture research on contemporary visionary architectural and urban activist practices in the South Bronx that refuse capitalist exploitation vis a vis New York City's economic transformation: from top-down public disinvestment and privatization to bottom-up self-provisioning and organizing. Through reading discussions, film/audiovisual analysis and mobilizing various tools of inquiry on the city, the seminar will learn from those involved in the long-term and

grassroots processes that have been redrawing the limits of socio-spatial organization in the South Bronx. The seminar will study the history of radical social movements from the second half of the 20th century in NYC with a special focus on the South Bronx. Groups of students will develop research and spatial visualizations of grassroots struggles for environmental and food justice, post-capitalist economic practices, public health, prison abolitionism and anti-gentrification. A short documentary film will be a collective deliverable for the seminar featuring interviews to NYC and South Bronx activists and residents, segments of existing movies and video recorded in our various seminar visits and meetings in the neighborhood. The work produced in the seminar will be included in the Architectures of Refusal platform which brings to focus the emancipatory spatial practices of social movements that oppose the neoliberal oligarchical status quo.

ARCH 712
Baroque Parameters
Andrew Saunders — 2019A

Deep plasticity and dynamism of form, space and light are explicit signatures of the Baroque Architecture; less obvious are the disciplined mathematical principles that generate these effects. Through art historians Rudolf Wittkower, Heinrich Wolfflin, and John Rupert Martin in addition to philosopher Gottfried Leibniz (via Gilles Deleuze), Robin Evans and the history of mathematics by Morris Kline, the course will examine how geometry and mathematics were integral to 17th-century science, philosophy, art, architecture and religion. The new revelation of a heliocentric universe, nautical navigation in the Age of Expansion, and the use of gunpowder spawned new operative geometry of elliptical paths, conic sections and differential equations. The geometric and political consequences of these advances are what link Baroque architects Francesco Borromini and Guarino Guarini to other great thinkers of the period including Decartes, Galileo, Kepler, Desargues, and Newton. Through the exploitation of trigonometric parameters of the arc and the chord, Baroque architects produced astonishing effects, performance and continuity. Generative analysis by parametric reconstruction and new speculative modeling will reexamine the base principles behind 17-century topology and reveal renewed relevance of the Baroque to the contemporary.

ARCH 714
Museum as Site: Critique, Intervention, and Production
Andrea Hornick — 2019A

In this course, we will take the museum as a site for critique, invention, and production. As architecture, cultural institution, and site of performance, the museum offers many relevant opportunities. Students will visit, analyze, and discuss a number of local exhibitions and produce their own intervention in individual or group projects. Exhibition design, design of museum, the process of curating, producing

artworks ranging from paintings to installation and performance, as well as attention to conservation, installation, museum education and the logistics and economics of exhibition will be discussed on site and in seminar. These topics and others will be open for students to engage as part of their own creative work produced for the class and an online exhibition.

ARCH 718
History and Theory of Architecture and Climate
Daniel Barber — 2019A

This seminar will explore the history of buildings as mechanisms of climate management and the theoretical and conceptual framework that pertain. From the 1930s to the 1960s, before mechanical systems of heating, ventilation and air conditioning (HVAC) were widely available, the design of a building—including relationship to site, use of shading devices and other systems, as well as familiar modernist tropes of open plans and an emphasis on volume—was central to managing seasonal and diurnal climatic variation. We will explore the history of these climate design strategies, and consider their significance to both the globalization of modern architecture and the conceptual frameworks that allow for discussion of design to resonate to changing geopolitical and geophysical conditions.

ARCH 719
Archigram and Its Legacy London, A Techtopia
Annette Fierro — 2018C

Acknowledging the ubiquitous proliferation of "Hi-Tech" architecture in contemporary London this research seminar examines the scope of technology as it emerges and re-emerges in the work of various architects currently dominating the city. This scope includes the last strains of post-war urbanism which spawned a legacy of radical architecture directly contributing to the Hi-Tech; a particular focus of the course be the contributing and contrasting influences provided by the counter-cultural groups of the 60's- Archigram, Superstudio, the Metabolists and others. Using the premise of Archigram's idea of infrastructure, both literal and of every the course will attempt to discover relational networks between works of the present day (Rogers, Foster, Grimshaw, etc.). As this work practices upon and within public space, an understanding of the contribution of technology urban theatricality will evolve which is relevant to contemporary spheres of technological design practices. Students will be required to produce and present a term research paper.

ARCH 720
Visual Literacy
Kutan Ayata — 2018C

The digital shift in disciplinary modes of design and visualization, resulted in a wide array of directions within the architectural discourse. It is no longer possible to locate any one representational medium as the locus of architectural thought as architecture can no longer be defined through the output of a single medium nor the mediums can be defined within the historical bounds of their terminologies. The reality of our discipline is that we work through collective mediums and conventions of drawings, models, images, simulations, texts, prototypes and buildings to visualize architectural concepts. This course will introduce the AAD majors to contemporary topics of visualization in architecture and explore multiple mediums of representation to help them gain the vital visual literacy to excel in the program. Students will be introduced to discursive background and current concepts of line drawing, fabricated object and constructed image.

ARCH 721
Designing Smart Objects for Play and Learning
saf Eshet — 2018C

ay's children enjoy a wide array of play
riences, with stories, learning, characters
games that exist as physical stand-alone
cts or toys enhanced with electronics or
ware. In this course, students will explore
domain of play and learning in order to
elop original proposals for new product ex-
ences that are at once tangible, immersive
dynamic. They will conduct research into
cation and psychology while also gaining
ds-on exposure to new product manifesta-
s in a variety of forms, both physical and
cal. Students will be challenged to work in
ns to explore concepts, share research and
d prototypes of their experiences in the
n of static objects that may have accom-
ying electronic devices or software. Final
gn proposals will consider future distribu-
models for product experiences such as 3D
ting, virtual reality and software- hardware
gration. Instruction will be part seminar
part workshop, providing research guid-
e and encouraging connections will subject
ter experts throughout the Penn campus.

ARCH 724
Immersive Kinematics/ Physical Computing: Body As Site
non Kim — 2018C

aim of this course is to understand the
medium of architecture within the format
research seminar. The subject matter of
media is to be examined and placed in a
plinary trajectory of building designed
construction technology that adapts to
erial and digital discoveries. We will also
d prototype with the new media, and es-
sh a disciplinary knowledge for ourselves.
seminar is interested in testing the
itecture-machine relationship, moving away
n architecture that looks like machines into
itecture that behaves like machines: An
lligence (based on the conceptual premise
project and in the design of a system), as
of a process (related to the generative
of architecture) and as the object itself and
mbedded intelligence.

ARCH 724
The Mathematics of Tiling in Architectural Design
shua Freese — 2019A

etition and difference in geometric tiling pat-
s produce visual complexity, intricacy, econo-
and articulation. From textiles and ceramics
rchitectural design, the tradition of tiling has
d from mathematical systems that inscribe
and three-dimensional geometric conditions,
nately yielding cultural effects that are unique
heir time. By examining this tradition across
and disciplines, this course will explore a
e of mathematical systems, tools, and media,
ell as how they advance contemporary archi-
ural topics such as parametrics, optimization,
ication, and implementation.

ARCH 725
Design Thinking
rah Rottenberg — 2018C

ating new product concepts was once a spe-
zed pursuit exclusively performed by design
essionals in isolation from the rest of an
nization. Today's products are developed
holistic process involving a collaboration
ng many disciplines. Design thinking - incor-
ating processes, approaches, and working
hods from traditional designers' toolkits—has

become a way of generating innovative ideas to
challenging problems and refining those ideas.
Rapid prototyping techniques, affordable and
accessible prototyping platforms, and an itera-
tive mindset have enabled people to more reli-
ably translate those ideas into implementable
solutions. In this course, students will be
exposed to these techniques and learn how to
engage in a human-centered design process.

ARCH 726
Furniture Design as Strategic Process
Mikael Avery, Brad Ascalon — 2018C

Like architecture, furniture exists at the
intersection of idea and physical form. Due
to the specific scale that furniture occupies,
however, this physical form relates not only to
the environment in which the furniture is set,
but also intimately to the physical bodies that
interact with and around it. Additionally, as a
manufactured product, often specified in large
quantities, furniture must also address not
only poetic considerations, but practical and
economic ones as well. Instead of being seen as
one-off objects, the furniture created in this
seminar focuses on furniture development as a
strategic design process where the designer's
role is to understand the various responsibilities to each stakeholder (client/manufacturer,
market/customer, environment) and the additional considerations (materials, processes,
manufacturability, etc.), and ultimately translate these points into a potentially successful
product. In order to approach furniture in this
manner, the course will be structured around
specific design briefs and clustered into three
distinct but continuous stages. First, through
focused research into stakeholder needs and
potential market opportunities, students will
craft tailored design proposals and development
concepts accordingly. Next, students will work
toward visualizing a concept, complete with
sketches, small mock-ups, scale-model prototypes, technical drawings, connections and other
pertinent details in order to refine their proposals and secure a real world understanding of the
manufacturing processes and the potential ob-
stacles created by their decisions. From insights
gained and feedback from these steps, students
will ultimately develop a final design proposal for
a piece, collection, or system of furniture that
successfully leverages their understanding of a
thoughtful and deliberate design strategy.

ARCH 727
Industrial Design I
Peter Bressler — 2019A

Industrial design (ID) is the professional service
of creating and developing concepts and specifications that optimize the function, value and
appearance of products and systems for the
mutual benefit of both user and manufacturer.
Industrial designers develop these concepts
and specifications through collection, analysis
and synthesis of user needs data guided by
the special requirements of the client or
manufacturer. They are trained to prepare
clear and concise recommendations through
drawings, models and verbal descriptions. The
profession has evolved to take its appropriate
place alongside Engineering and Marketing as
one of the cornerstones of Integrated Product
Design teams. The core of Industrial Design's
knowledge base is a mixture of fine arts, commercial arts and applied sciences utilized with a
set of priorities that are firstly on the needs of
the end user and functionality, then the market
and manufacturing criteria. This course will
provide an overview and understanding of the
theories, thought processes and methodologies employed in the daily practice of Industrial
Design. This includes understanding of ethno-
graphic research and methodologies, product
problem solving, creative visual communication,

human factors/ergonomics application and
formal and surface development in product
scale. This course will not enable one to become
an industrial designer but will enable one to understand and appreciate what industrial design
does, what it can contribute to society and why
it is so much fun.

ARCH 731
Experiments in Structure
Mohamad Al Khayer — 2018C

This course studies the relationships between
geometric space and those structural systems
that amplify tension. Experiments using the
hand (touch and force) in coordination with the
eye (sight and geometry) will be done during the
construction and observation of physical models. Verbal, mathematical and computer models
are secondary to the reality of the physical
model. However these models will be used to
give dimension and document the experiments.
Team reports will serve as interim and final
examinations. In typology, masonry structures
in compression (e.g., vault and dome) correlate
with "Classical" space, and steel or reinforced
concrete structures in flexure (e.g., frame, slab
and column) with "Modernist" space. We seek
the spatial correlates to tensile systems of
both textiles (woven or braided fabrics where
both warp and weft are tensile), and baskets
(where the warp is tensile and the weft is compressive). In addition to the experiments, we
will examine Le Ricolais' structural models held
by the Architectural Archives.

ARCH 732
Daylighting
Jessica Zofchak — 2018C, 2019A

This course aims to introduce fundamental
daylighting concepts and tools to analyze day-
lighting design. The wide range of topics to be
studied includes site planning, building envelope
and shading optimization, passive solar design,
daylight delivery methods, daylight analysis
structure and results interpretation, and a
brief daylighting and lighting design integration.

ARCH 732
Material and Structural Intelligence
Mark Nicol, Sameer Kumar — 2018C

The semester long project will involve a gradual
development of architectural ideas that are intimately informed by and centered on knowledge
of Structure and Materiality. Employing both
physical and digital simulations, the students
will synthesize knowledge acquired in previous
courses in structures, materials, and construction methods to develop architectural solutions
within a carefully selected set of determinants.

ARCH 732
Geometric Structural Design
Masoud Akbarzadeh — 2018C

Geometric structural design provides a com-
prehensive introduction to novel geometric
methods of structural design based on 2D and
3D graphical statics. The primary emphasis
of the course will be on developing a general
understanding of the relationship between
structural forms in equilibrium and the geometric representation of their internal and
external forces. This link is the main apparatus
for designing provocative structural forms
using only geometric techniques rather than
complicated algebraic/numerical methods.
Moreover, special consideration will be given to
materialization of the structural geometry and
the proper fabrication techniques to construct
the complex geometry of the structure.

ARCH 732
Matter and Energy
Franca Trubiano — 2018C

This seminar/workshop promotes architectural innovation in the field of construction technology. Matter + Energy are the two fields of enquiry which guide and structure the course's reading seminars and prototype workshops. Students will design and fabricate building related prototypes that productively respond to a well-documented and socially relevant environmental need. The creative and critical integration of Matter + Energy is the ambition of each prototype. Materials such as films, composites and plastic/polymers will be central to the investigation, as will the energy related topics of thermodynamics, light/heat studies and renewable energies. Invited design and building industry professionals will advise student teams and offer critical reviews of their process during the semester. Lastly, students will be introduced to performance design metrics used in evaluating the environmental impact of their material and energy choices, be they embodied energy, carbon emissions, or Life Cycle Assessments.

More specifically, the seminar is dedicated to the development of a body of knowledge aligned with socially relevant ecological design principles. Students are encouraged to design and prototype innovative solutions for housing the world's homeless. The physical constraints of the art of building are essential to the exercise when the construction of new technologies is positioned between the practice points of energy + matter; power and materials.

Given the world's energy resources are limited and fair acquisition is impossible given corporate and governmental power dynamics, the design of basic shelter for hundreds of millions of homeless must address this basic lack of fuel. Seeking inventive applications in renewable energy in the design of minimum existence housing is one goal of this seminar; the other, the innovative and intelligent application of materials to the same end. Students working in teams will develop their own Energy + Matter equation, actualizing a world of ideas and fabrication practices which give rise to socially relevant zero energy building prototypes.

ARCH 732
Enclosures: Selection, Affinities & Integration
Charles Jay Berman — 2019A

Details should be considered in the traditional sense, as assemblages of constituent elements. Not as a mere collection of parts, rather as an "assemblage," the act of assembling under a guiding principle; the relationship to a whole. Frascari defines the detail as the union of construction—having the dual role of ruling both the construction and construing of architecture. This obligation of the relationship of the parts to the whole and the whole to the parts is the essence of the revelatory detail in service of architecture. This seminar seeks to establish a framework of understanding enclosures in this sense of the revelatory detail. We will seek to counterpoint the numerical (external) facts of what is accepted as facade design (criteria, codes, loads, forces and consumptions) with an understanding of the generative processes underlying these physical criteria. The aim of this seminar is to arm the student with a guided understanding of the materials and assemblies available to them to form enclosures. The underlying intent is twofold. In a generative role as architects, the course intends not for an encyclopedic overview of the elements and calculative methodologies of envelope design. Rather we will endeavor to investigate concepts of enclosure through assemblage of elements, mediated by details, in the service of the architectural intentions of the student. In an execution role as architects in practice, the investigation into methodologies of deploy-ment and execution of enclosure, materials and assemblies is intended to arm the students to engage proactively in their future practices with the succession of consulting engineers, specialty facade consultants, manufacturers and facade contractors that they will encounter during the execution of their work.

ARCH 732
Advanced Production
Masoud Akbarzadeh — 2019A

The course intends to address the challenges in the design development process and fabrication of the Tiny House concept developed in the fall studio. The primary objectives include ensuring the structural integrity of the prefab systems, sealing strategies and the necessary foundation for the structure, meticulous detailing the interior and exterior of the house, overcoming the fabrication challenges, and defining the assembly logic/sequence to complete the house. To achieve these goals, the students will design the assembly mechanisms for prefab systems and the junction between the glazing and the concrete. Also, they will investigate on the material transition from exterior to the interior and will provide solutions to include furniture, equipment, and embedded lighting within the modules. The outcome of the course will consist of the complete construction document for the whole house and a one-to-one scale prototype of minimum three assembled modules to reflect the solutions for the challenges of building the tiny house.

ARCH 732
Deployable Structures
Mohamad Al Khayer — 2019A

The objective of this course is to introduce the rapidly growing field of deployable structures through hands on experiments conducted in workshop environments. Students develop skills in making deployable structures.

ARCH 732
Principles of Digital Fabrication
Mikael Avery — 2019A

Through the almost seamless ability to output digital designs to physical objects, digital fabrication has transformed the way designers work. At this point, many of the tools and techniques of digital fabrication are well established and almost taken for granted within the design professions. To begin this course, we will review these "traditional" digital fabrication techniques in order to establish a baseline skill set to work from. We will then explore hybrid approaches to digital fabrication in which multiple techniques are utilized within the same work. During all of these exercises we will discuss the development of 3D printing and its place in the digital fabrication dialogue.

ARCH 732
Heavy Architecture
Philip Ryan — 2019A

Heavy Architecture is a seminar that will examine buildings that, through their tectonics or formal expression, connote a feeling of weight, permanence, or "heaviness." Analysis of these buildings and methods of construction stand in relation to the proliferation of thin, formally exuberant and, by virtue of their use or commodified nature, transient buildings. The course is not a rejection or formal critique of "thin" architecture, but instead an analysis of the benefits and drawbacks of the "heavy" building type in terms of a building's financial, environmental, symbolic or conceptual, and functional goals. The course will parse the alleged nostalgic or habitual reputation of "heavy" architecture within the context of architecture's ongoing struggle to be the vanguard of the built environment even while its relevancy and voice is challenged by economic, stylistic, and social forces.

ARCH 734
Ecological Architecture: Contemporary Practices
Todd Woodward — 2019A

Architecture is an inherently exploitive act—take resources from the earth and produce waste and pollution when we construct and operate buildings. As global citizens, we have an ethical responsibility to minimize these negative impacts. As creative professionals, however, we have a unique ability to go farther than simply being "less bad." We are learning design in ways that can help heal the damage and regenerate our environment. This course explores these evolving approaches to design from neo-indigenous to eco-tech to LEED to biomimicry to living buildings. Taught by a practicing architect with many years of experience designing green buildings, the course also features guest lecturers from complementary fields—landscape architects, hydrologists, recycling contractors and materials specialists. Coursework includes in-class discussion, short essays and longer research projects.

ARCH 736
Building Acoustics
Joseph Solway — 2019A

This course covers the fundamentals of architectural acoustics and the interdependence between acoustics and architectural design. The course explores the effects of materials and room shape on sound absorption, reflection and transmission, and demonstrates how modeling, visualization and auralization can be used to understand acoustic and aid the design process. The course includes a lecture on the history and future of performance space design, a visit to the Arup SoundLab in New York and two assignments, one practical (Boom Box) and one theoretical (Sound Space).

ARCH 736
Water Shaping Architecture
Stuart Mardeusz, Jonathan Weiss — 2019A

Without water, there is no life. Water impacts, influences and shapes architecture in many different aspects. This course covers a range of subjects including; the physics of water, the systems to gather, distribute, supply and treat potable water, grey water, waste water, including the correlation to energy and recycling that are integrated into the architecture of buildings. How do our choices as architects impact access to water, and how are those issues predetermined on a building, local, regional and continental scale? If Sustainability is about providing for our needs while allowing for future generations to do the same, how does our outlook on water shape our decision-making process?

ARCH 736
Architectural Workflows in the Design and Delivery of Buildings
Richard Garber — 2019A

This seminar in design and technology would focus on the concept of the architectural workflow as it pertains to both contemporary operations in design practice as well as novel project delivery methods. The synthesis of digital design platforms with simulation and increasing access to data in the form of natural phenomena, ecology, and building performance has allowed contemporary architects to engage the notion of workflows with others in design

d construction practices. Beyond design
ent and process, workflows occupy an ex-
nded territory within architectural practice
d merge digital design operations with con-
uction activities, project delivery, and post-
cupation scenarios in both virtual and actual
mats. The implications for the architecture,
gineering and construction (AEC) industry
uld not be greater, and these new collabora-
e models have become as important as the
vel buildings they allow us to produce.

ARCH 736
BIM (Building Information Modeling): Virtual Construction and Detailing
anca Trubiano — 2019A

M has become the lingua franca of building.
ring the past decade, significant changes
ve taken place in the nature of design and
nstruction practices which has transformed
e very nature of architectural representa-
n. Architects no longer draw depictions
that which they intend for others to build;
ther, they model, code, simulate, data-scape,
d integrate that which they virtually build
ngside their colleague and collaborators
gineers and builders. The production of
ormation rich virtual BIM models is the
ound upon which all construction activities
advanced and complex multi-story build-
s takes place. BIM is also at the origins of
ntemporary innovations in Integrated Design,
e creation of collaborative platforms which
n to maximize the sustainable outcomes in
e project delivery of buildings. Moreover,
ng able to collaboratively produce, share,
d query a Building Information Model renders
ssible the global practice of design and con-
uction. The course will familiarize students
this important field of architectural practice.

ARCH 737
Semi-Fictious Realms
hristopher McAdams — 2018C

e pursuit of immersive digital experiences
s long been a goal of the computing industry.
rly wearable displays designed in the 1960s
picted simple three-dimensional graphics in
ys that had never been seen before. Through
al and error, digital pioneers reframed the
ationship between user and machine, and
er the last five decades, have made strides
at advanced both the input and output
chanisms we are so comfortable with today.
a field, architecture has been reliant on
ese advancements to design and docu-
nt buildings, but these tools still leave the
hitect removed from the physicality of the
sign, with their work depicted as 2D lines or
planes alone. This course will study the evo-
ionary advancements made that now allow
to fully inhabit digital worlds through Virtual
ality. Using the HTC Vive and Unreal Engine,
dents will generate immersive, photorealis-
models of unbuilt architectural works and
lore digital/physical interactivity. From the
races of Paul Rudolph's Lower Manhattan
ressway to Boullee s Cenotaph for Newton,
goal of this course is to breathe new life
o places and spaces that have, until this
e, never been built or occupied.

ARCH 739
New Approaches to an Architecture of Health
kael Avery — 2018C

alth care is taking on a new role in our soci-
— with a refocusing from episodic care for
se who are ill or symptomatic to providing
-long care geared towards maintaining well-
s. These changes are evident across numer-
areas of design, from wearable technologies

that track and analyze, to large scale building
initiatives that aim to create healthier environments and improve lives through strategic
planning initiatives.

A concrete, physical representation of this
paradigm shift can be found within the hospital
building itself and in the new manner in which
hospitals are looking to serve their patients and
care for their clinicians. Simultaneously both
public and private spaces, hospitals are complex
systems in which sickness, health, hospitality,
technology, emergency, and community share
space and compete for resource.

In order to frame our present day understanding of the role of architecture (and design)
in fostering health for individuals and within
communities, this seminar will begin with an
exploration of the historical and contemporary
perspectives on the role of the architect and
built environment on health. (Parallels between
design and our ever-changing understanding of
the biological, social, and environmental causes
of sickness and disease will also be explored.)
During this conversation, students will read
articles and study recently constructed projects
in order to examine the ways in which the architects approached these topics through built
form. Following from this foundation, students
will craft arguments for a new approach to the
individual, the community, health, and architecture through a written response and architecturally designed scenario that argues for their
perspective on how architecture can and should
shape the health of those who inhabit it.

ARCH 741
Archicture Design Innovation
Ali Rahim — 2018C

The mastery of techniques, whether in design,
production or both, does not necessarily yield
great architecture. As we all know, the most
advanced techniques can still yield average
designs. Architects are becoming increasingly
adept producing complexity & integrating
digital design and fabrication techniques into
their design process—yet there are few truly
elegant projects. Only certain projects that are
sophisticated at the level of technique achieve
elegance. This seminar explores some of the
instances in which designers are able to move
beyond technique, by commanding them to
such a degree so as to achieve elegant aesthetics within the formal development of projects.

ARCH 742
Function of Fashion in Architecture
Danielle Willems — 2019A

The Function of Fashion in Architecture will survey the history of fashion and the architectural
parallels starting from Ancient Civilization to
Present. The focus will be on the relevance of
garment design, methods and techniques and
their potential to redefine current architecture
elements such as envelope, structure, seams,
tectonics and details. The functional, tectonic and
structural properties of garment design will be
explored as generative platforms to conceptualize very specific architectural elements. One of
the challenges in the course is the re-invention
of a means of assessment, the development of
notations and techniques that will document the
forces and the production of difference in the
spatial manifestations of the generative systems.

ARCH 743
Form and Algorithm
Cecil Balmond and Ezio Blasetti — 2018C

The critical parameter will be to develop the
potential beyond finite forms of explicit and
parametric modeling towards non-linear algorithmic processes. We will seek novel patterns

of organizatio, structure, and articulation as
architectural expressions within the emergent
properties of feedback loops and rule based
systems. This seminar will accommodate both
introductory and advanced levels. No previous
scripting experience is necessary. It will consist
of a series of introductory sessions, obligatory
intensive workshops, lectures followed by
suggested readings, and will gradually focus on
individual projects. Students will be encouraged
to investigate the limits of algorithmic design
both theoretically and in practice through a
scripting environment.

ARCH 744
Digital Fabrication
Ferda Kolatan — 2019A

As we have entered a postdigital era, the domi-
nance of a purely technological approach as a vehicle for design innovation has waned. Questions
of substance and disciplinary autonomy have
found their way back into the contemporary
cultural discourse, enriching the way we examine
and deploy advanced technologies towards novel
expressions in architecture. This seminar will investigate, through the production of estranged
objects, opportunities for design that are being
generated at the intersection of machinic and
human minds, and speculate on possible futures
in which concepts of nature and technology have
been inseparably intertwined.

ARCH 746
Cinema and Architecture in Translation
Danielle Willems, Nicholas Klein — 2019A

Cinema and Architecture in Translation is a
seminar that will survey key cinematic moments and techniques within the history of film
and find new intersections between architecture and narratives. The focus will be on the
relevance of mise-en-scene, the background
and building figures of architecture and future
speculations of the city, yet in relation to narrative dynamics. One of the challenges in considerations and techniques that will affect both
conceptualization and the production of spatial
manifestations using potent visual platforms.
Current pre and post-production techniques
in film making methods are converging with
architectural digital representation. This is
an opportunity that provides fertile ground
for architects to re-examine the "digital" in a
variety of scales in relation to impactful narratives and visualizations. These tools, specifically the technique of "matte-painting" will be
explored in this course. There is a rich history
in constructing images, speculative worlds and
scenes for the film industry. We will explore the
parallels between the tools and strategies of
cinematic visualization as it relates to advanced
architectural image making. Students will have
the opportunity to analyze filmic scene making,
learn advanced representation and techniques
in matte painting and zbrush. Above all this
course will engage students in the conceptual
as well as practical complementarities of architecture and cinema, while watching some of the
best films ever made and the most provocative
and insightful books to help process them.
An important aspect of this course will be to
explore the differences between "real" archi-

texture and the cinematic architecture. The expansive Space and Time in which cinematic architecture is located, creates an incubator where true innovated speculation can occur. This is an advanced representation course that produces 2D images and narrative texts.

ARCH 748
Architecture and the New Elegance
Hina Jamelle — 2019A

This design seminar will define and elaborate on the following topics for the digital discourse—the contemporary diagram, technique, structural thinking, systemic thinking and aesthetic projections. Technological innovations establish new status quos and updated platforms from which to operate and launch further innovations. Design research practices continually reinvent themselves and the techniques they use to stay ahead of such developments. Reinvention can come through techniques that have already been set in motion. Mastery of techniques remains important and underpins the use of digital technologies in the design and manufacturing of elegant buildings. But, ultimately, a highly sophisticated formal language propels aesthetics. The repositioning of design intent and the complex order generated by the behavioral techniques of multi-agent systems has implications for the affects which are generated as well as the nature of hierarchy within architecture. The distributed non-linear operation of swarm systems intrinsically resists the discrete articulation of hierarchies within Modern architecture and contemporary parametric component logic. The bottom-up nature of swarm systems refocuses tectonic concerns on the assemblage at the micro scale rather than the sequential subdivision of program or form. The seminar will explore strategies for high population agent models through the use of lightweight algorithmic environments, in particular the Java-based platform Processing.

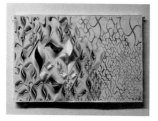

ARCH 750
Parafictional Objects
Kutan Ayata — 2019A

This representation/design seminar explores the aesthetics of estrangement in realism through various mediums. The reality of the discipline is that architecture is a post-medium effort. Drawings, Renderings, Models, Prototypes, Computations, Simulations, Texts, and Buildings are all put forward by architects as a speculative proposal for the reality of the future. Students will explore the reconfiguration of a "found object" in multiple mediums and represent parafictional scenarios in various techniques of realism. At a time when rendering engines enable the production of hyper-realistic images within the discipline without any critical representational agenda, it has become ever more imperative to rigorously speculate on realism.

ARCH 751
Ecology, Technology, and Design
William Braham — 2018C

This course will examine the ecological nature of design at a range of scales, from the most

intimate aspects of product design to the largest infrastructures, from the use of water in bathroom to the flow of traffic on the highway. It is a first principle of ecological design that everything is connected, and that activities at one scale can have quite different effects at other scales, so the immediate goal of the course will be to identify useful and characteristic modes of analyzing the systematic, ecological nature of design work, from the concept of the ecological footprint to market share. The course will also draw on the history and philosophy of technology to understand the particular intensity of contemporary society, which is now characterized by the powerful concept of the complex, self-regulating system. The system has become both the dominant mode of explanation and the first principle of design and organization.

ARCH 752
MEBD Research SEminar
William Braham — 2018C

Environmental building design is a process of discovery, of understanding what to work on, before it ever becomes a matter of design or of performance analysis. This means tackling questions large and small, considering both technical details and architectural possibilities, and establishing a position in a continually evolving field. The work of the seminar is to develop methods of research for this complex field, to develop tools, information, and concepts to guide design. The course will help students establish research habits and agendas to support their work in environmental building design, both in design studios and in practice. That work will be developed in stages through the semester. Beginning with case studies of exemplary environmental buildings students will explore specific topics in building science and technology as they contribute to architectural projects, developing bibliographies of current work and a final research report, summarizing the state of the field and current tools and practices.

ARCH 753
Building Performance Simulation
Efrie Escott — 2018C

Simulation is the process of making a simplified model of a complex system to better predict or understand the behavior or the original system. This course provides students with an understanding of building design simulation methods, hands-on experience in using digital and physical simulation models, and exploration of the technologies, underlying principles, and potential applications of simulation tools in architecture through weekly lectures and hands-on simulation lab exercises. A series of analysis projects will link design decision-making to building performance outcomes.

ARCH 762
Design and Development
Jaime Flaherty — 2019A

This course introduces the relationship between architectural design and real estate development. Following a discussion of fundamentals, examples focus on commercial building types, and illustrate how architectural design can contribute to real estate development. Topics include housing design commercial buildings, adaptive reuse, downtown development, mixed-use projects, and planned communities.

ARCH 765
Project Management
Charles Capaldi — 2018C, 2019A

This course is an introduction to construction management, project management and various construction project delivery systems. In the

study of construction delivery systems, we will examine the players, relationships and the advantages and disadvantages of different contractual and practical relationships, both on the construction site and at the tops of the various "paper piles." Exercises and lectures will focus on developing perspectives into the various roles, needs and expectations of the many parties involved in a construction project and the management skills and techniques which help to bring a project to a successful conclusion.

ARCH 768
Real Estate Development
Alan Feldman — 2018C
Asuka Nakahara — 2019A

This course evaluates "ground-up" development as well as re-hab, re-development, and acquisition investments. We examine raw and developed land and the similarities and differences of traditional real estate product types including office, R & D, retail, warehouses, single family and multi-family residential, mixed use, and land as well as "specialty" uses like golf courses, assisted living, and fractional share ownership. Emphasis is on concise analysis and decision making. We discuss the development process with topics including market analysis, site acquisition, due diligence, zoning, entitlements, approvals, site planning, building design, construction, financing, leasing, and ongoing management and disposition. Special topics like workouts and running a development company are also discussed. Course lessons apply to all markets but the class discusses US markets only. Throughout the course, we focus on risk management and leadership issues. Numerous guest lecturers who are leaders in the real estate industry participate in the learning process.

ARCH 771
Professional Practice II
Philip Ryan — 2018C

This course examines the issues and processes involved in running a professional architectural practice and designing buildings in the contemporary construction environment. It will build on the knowledge of the project process gained in Professional Practice I to examine the way in which an office is "designed" to facilitate the execution of design and construction. Issues of finance, liability, ethics, and the codes that overlay atop the design and construction industry will be discussed. The lectures will draw connections between the student's studio design knowledge to date and the instructor's experience in practice including local building examples and guest lectures by relevant professionals. Guests from within the field of architecture and construction (and outside occasionally) will round out the semester lectures.

ARCH 811
Architecture's Cultural Performance: The Façade
David Leatherbarrow — 2018C

This course will reconsider these alternatives and ask again about the interrelationships between topics of design that seem to be categorically distinct: the project's functionality and its style, its provision of settings that allow the enactment of practical purposes and its contribution to the image and appearance of our landscapes and cities. Our concentration will be at once historical and thematic. We will study and reconsider buildings from the twentieth century and we will ask questions that resonate through the past several decades into the present, questions about the building (its materials, construction, and figuration) as well as the process of design (description, projection, and discovery). Throughout the course we will return to the building's most visible and articulate surface: the façade.

ARCH 814
Idea of the Avant-Garde
an Ockman — 2019A

historian of architecture has written as
ensely about the contradictions of archi-
ture in late-modern society or reflected
deeply on the resulting problems and tasks
architectural historiography as Manfredo
uri (1935-1994). For many, the Italian his-
ian's dismissal of "hopes in design" under
ditions of advanced capitalism produced a
ciplinary impasse. This in turn led to call to
lier Tafuri-to move beyond his pessimis-
and lacerating stance. The seminar will
dertake a close reading of one of Tafuri's
st complexly conceived and richly elaborated
oks, The Sphere and the Labyrinth: Avant-
rdes and Architecture form Piranesi to the
'0s. We shall also read a number of primary
d secondary sources on the historical con-
ts under discussion and consider a number
mportant intertexts that shed light on
uri's position. The objectives of the course
at once historical and historiographic: we
ll we shall be concerned both with actual
ents and with how they have been written
o history. Finally, we shall reassess the role
an avant-garde in architecture and compare
uri's conception to that advanced in other
ciplines. Is the concept of an avant-garde
ll viable today? Or should it be consigned to
dustbin of twentieth-century ideas?

CREDITS

CREDITS & ACKNOWLEDGEMENTS

Publishers of Architecture, Art, and Design
Gordon Goff: Publisher

www.oroeditions.com
info@oroeditions.com

Published by ORO Editions

Design:
WSDIA | WeShouldDoItAll (wsdia.com)
Typefaces: Founders Grotesk Text designed by Kris Sowersby of Klim Type Foundry

Editorial Team:
Winka Dubbeldam, Professor and Chair
Scott Loeffler, Department Coordinator
Ivy Gray-Klein, Events and Publications Coordinator

Copy Editor:
Ivy Gray-Klein, Scott Loeffler, Sarah Lam

ORO Project Coordinator: Kirby Anderson

10 9 8 7 6 5 4 3 2 1 First Edition

Library of Congress data available upon request. World Rights: Available

ISBN: 978-1-943532-31-5

Color Separations and Printing: ORO Group Ltd.
Printed in China.

International Distribution: www.oroeditions.com/distribution

ORO Editions makes a continuous effort to minimize the overall carbon footprint of its publications. As part of this goal, ORO Editions, in association with Global ReLeaf, arranges to plant trees to replace those used in the manufacturing of the paper produced for its books. Global ReLeaf is an international campaign run by American Forests, one of the world's oldest nonprofit conservation organizations. Global ReLeaf is American Forests' education and action program that helps individuals, organizations, agencies, and corporations improve the local and global environment by planting and caring for trees.